UFO

COLD CASES:

MISSOURI

SECRET USAF FILES
1952-1968

DECLASSIFIED

By Dave Toplikar

UFO Cold Cases: Missouri, *Secret USAF Files, 1952-1968, De-classified.*

ISBN-13: 978-1726495813

Graphics and cover illustration by the author

TABLE OF CONTENTS

Acknowledgements   5

About this book . . .   7

PART I: **MISSOURI FLAP**   11

1. **An alien armada?**   13

2. **Green UFO over KC**   37

PART 2: **The WAVE OF 1954**   47

3. **Lights over St. Louis**   49

4. **Butler's lights**   65

5. **Baffling boomerang**   75

PART 3: **FEAR & FANTASY**   91

6. **A dozen disks**   93

7. **Disabling a car**   107

PART 4: **CRITICISM MOUNTS**   119

8. **A secret spy program?**   121

9. **Burning red orb**   133

10. **UFO cattle drive?**   147

EPILOGUE   173

About the Author   179

Acknowledgements

My thanks go out to the many UFO researchers from years past and their organizations who took it upon themselves to keep tabs on the U.S. Air Force **Project Blue Book** documents and eventually make them available online for study.

Thanks to my wife, Diane; my son, Matt; my daughters, Katy, Bonnie and Julie, for inspiring me to move forward on this project.

Thanks to my relatives and friends for telling me about their own UFO sightings and encouraging me in this effort. I was surprised how many people had seen them, but not reported them for fear of ridicule.

Thanks also to Joel Sanderson for keeping me moving on this project.

About this book . . .

No, as in my first book published in 2016, I still haven't seen a flying saucer, a UFO (unidentified flying object), a UAP (unidentified aerial phenomenon) or seen anything in the sky I couldn't explain.

But as a longtime journalist in the Kansas City area and in Las Vegas, others have told me their own UFO stories. I have taken phone calls from serious people who wanted to report UFOs.

They wanted to know what that strange thing was they saw floating above the trees. Or those strange lights they saw. Or, in Las Vegas, that strange flying cylinder that was being followed by three black helicopters. They wanted answers. And they thought somebody should know about it.

Over the years since the late 1970s, I've made phone calls to sheriff's offices, to police departments, and even to Air Force officials. Just about every official joked about it. No one seemed to ever want to take UFO sightings seriously. A lot of people feared ridicule for reporting them. They still do.

But there was a time when one government entity was openly serious about UFOs — the U.S Air Force.

It began with sightings of lights or unknown objects in the mid 1940s, intensifying in 1947. U.S. military officials were worried about protecting our air space.

So for more than two decades — from about 1947 to 1969 — the Air Force investigated and/or documented more than 12,000 sightings.

The thousands of investigations were part of classified operations first informally called **"Project Saucer."** Those sightings were merged into an operation called **Project Sign**, which then became **Project Grudge** and eventually **Project Blue Book**.

But the Air Force is now out of the *public* UFO business.

When the Air Force ended **Project Blue Book** in 1969, it claimed to have never found any actual physical evidence of UFOs, or found them to be a threat to the country.

The vast majority of the reports were explained away as misinterpretations of everyday objects: a bird, a balloon, ball lightning, swamp gas or tricks of the imagination.

However, among those 12,000-plus cases were 701 that were classified as "unknowns" — cases that defied any conventional explanation. The Air Force refused to publicly speculate any of the "unknowns" might be extraterrestrial. These unknown cases gathered dust for many years. They were mostly forgotten, except by UFO researchers. But over time these cold cases were shared online. I first became interested in some of the online cases in my hometown area around Kansas City.

My research led to a 2016 book: **UFO Cold Cases: Kansas** *(available on **amazon.com**)*. I was surprised at the responses to that book as I spoke to groups around Kansas. People are still seeing them. The mystery is still very much unresolved.

For the last year, I've been checking into similar baffling sightings from old **Project Blue Book** from Missouri that were marked as "unknown." These were once "classified," real-life X-files, but are now public.

I was disappointed an alleged 1941 UFO crash in Cape Girardeau, Missouri was not part of **Project Blue Book**.

Over the years, news accounts have laid out the Cape Girardeau event allegedly told by a minister on his deathbed: The minister claimed to have been summoned by police to come with them to a bad nighttime aircraft crash to provide last rites to the victims. Upon arriving, they found alien bodies and a crashed disc-shaped craft with strange markings. The minister and local first responders looked on as the Army came in and took the aliens and their craft, and swore everyone to secrecy.

However the alleged July 1941 Cape Girardeau UFO case, like the Roswell, New Mexico, event six years later in 1947, were not documented and archived in the military's **Project Blue Book** cases.

Researchers looking into the Cape Girardeau local legend have pieced the story together based on witnesses who came forward years later, in the 1980s. Hopefully documentation exists, including photos, and will someday be revealed.

Until then, we do have documentation of hundreds of formerly classified Missouri sightings, including several unexplained cold cases retold in this book.

As I was finishing my research of these decades-old Missouri cases, in December 2017 some major news organizations broke a stunning story — after all these years, we know for certain the military is still chasing UFOs.

The Pentagon is still serious about them, just not openly. The Pentagon spent $22 million from 2007 to 2012 to study whether UAPs (unidentified aerial phenomenon) were a threat or whether they can offer any new aviation technology. The **New York Times** even released formerly classified videos of UFOs that baffled the pilots who gave chase. They could disappear from sight. They could not be challenged.

Those recent modern-day military sightings, plus my own research into the following Missouri UFO cold cases, make me believe that we need to rethink our attitudes toward this subject. UFO sightings haven't gone away. Something is out there.

I think it's time for the government, the scientific community and the public to treat UFOs seriously and with transparency. Please review these cold case accounts with an open but skeptical mind. Maybe you'll agree.

— *Dave Toplikar, September 2018*

PART I:

MISSOURI FLAP

In 1947, the U.S. Air Force was charged with investigating reports of "flying saucers" by the military and civilians. "**Project Saucer**," the informal name used by the news media of the classified project, was formalized into **Project Sign** and later into **Project Grudge**. The growing public concern over flying saucers led the Air Force to reorganize its investigation in late 1951 into **Project Blue Book** under Capt. Edward Ruppelt.

Sightings rose in the spring of 1952. They culminated in July 1952, when UFOs were reportedly seen on two weekends in the night sky and on radar around the nation's Capitol, an event UFO researchers call the "**Washington Flap**."

The first two chapters in this book cover two unexplained Missouri sightings from **Project Blue Book's** declassified files that took place in roughly the same time period as the Washington Flap.

1. An alien armada?

KIRKSVILLE, Missouri (July 12, 1952) — No outside witnesses ever came forward. As far as we know, no one reported hearing anything unusual.

But right around 9 p.m. — about the time the last light was dimming, the crickets began to chirp and the fireflies darted about — some objects quite out of the ordinary entered the skies above northeast Missouri and southeast Iowa.

The first one showed up as a large white blob on what was in 1952, the Air Force's new state-of-the-art radar tracking screens at Kirksville, Missouri.

Another sweep of the radar arm showed the object on the glowing, greenish oscilloscope screen was moving fast — extremely fast.

Then a second strange object appeared. Then a third.

One by one, as the radar continued to sweep around the tracking screens, a total of six unidentified objects, in the form of white "blips" or "paint," were appearing on the screens' upper left.

The mysterious objects were moving to the right on the screens, or east, at an alarming rate. They were much faster than a flock of birds. They were many times faster than any planes known to be in the area.

Everyone around the radar screens took notice: the objects were clocked at 1,500 mph — more than twice the speed of sound.

Some of the men on duty rushed outside on that midsummer Saturday night. They couldn't make anything out visually in the fading twilight. They couldn't hear anything.

Back at the radar screens, the concern was growing. Could they be a threat? Were they incoming intercontinental ballistic missiles from the Soviet Union? Could they be meteors?

Or were they something else — something not necessarily from this planet, time period or dimension? Were they flying saucers?

It's been nearly six and a half decades since that unknown fleet or air armada streaked across this former Air Force base in northeast Missouri. Officially, it still remains unsolved.

Or was it? Have we been kept in the dark because of national security for more than six decades? If we have, why?

Reviewing Project Blue Book

The Kirksville radar sighting was one of the 701 cold cases that was never explained in **Project Blue Book**, the U.S. Air Force's longtime UFO investigation.

Project Blue Book ended in 1969 after cataloging 12,618 sightings. The Air Force put out an official statement saying investigators never found evidence UFOs were a threat to national security. They also claimed to have never found anything to make them think the "unknowns" were extraterrestrial — including any wreckage or alien bodies.

However, since 1969, many UFO researchers believe **Project Blue Book** was set up merely as the public face of what has been an on-going series of secret investigations into our military's encounters with UFOs since the early 1940s.

The government involvement began with Cold War national security efforts. Internal "need to know" compartmental policies and bureaucratic structures restricted information access across agencies. Even presidents couldn't cut through the secrecy maze. Also, some researchers have concluded the CIA used the flying saucer phenomenon to conduct its own disinformation and propaganda efforts.

Over time, the truth about what the military and our government's spy agencies know about UFOs has been obscured. That incomplete record has fed a growing number of conspiracy theories.

As a journalist, I'm wary about buying into conspiracy claims. I wanted to see the evidence for myself.

So when I learned many of the old **Blue Book** case files had been put online for study by the **National Investigations Committee on Aerial Phenomena**, NICAP.org, I started going through the documents myself.

As a newspaper reporter, I was very familiar with similar public documents dealing with traffic accidents or crimes. I used them regularly to construct news stories from the basic facts investigators jotted down on their standard forms. I found the **Project Blue Book** documents to be similar.

Generally the information from the early years of the **Blue Book** files is very good.

The summaries seem professional and they often have sketches — a lot more information than I would have expected. But can you trust what's in there?

A noticeable odor

As I've been looking through the documents, I've taken it a step further than merely studying the information. Given all the skepticism from many more modern UFO researchers, I try to see if the conclusions reached in these cold cases meet the "smell test."

That's a term I borrowed from journalism scholar John McManus' article titled "*Don't Be Fooled: Use the SMELL Test to Separate Fact from Fiction Online*" on the website mediashift.org to explain what I mean:

Was the Source reliable or did they have some other Motivation? Did the investigators give the Evidence enough attention? Should they have Logically talked to more people?

Or does the case smell a little fishy — where a reasonable person most likely thought they reached an evaluation too quickly, with too little evidence. What did they Leave behind unexamined?

Under McManus' smell test, some of the **Blue Book** cases have a noticeable odor.

For example, some of the so-called "identified" **Blue Book** cases were explained away as meteors or planets when the witness description clearly indicates something else.

And that raises some questions I hoped someday to resolve. Was **Project Blue Book** merely a public facade for the real UFO investigation?

Could some of the unexplained cases have been handed to spy agencies like the CIA or the National Reconnaissance Office? Were the investigators covering for our own secret projects?

Did the CIA fake sightings in some psychological game with the Russians? Have we been subjected to nearly 70 years of disinformation?

An invasion in 1952?

If you've watched some of the TV documentaries on UFOs or aliens, you've probably seen references to 1952 as being a big year for UFO sightings.

It's often called the "1952 flap" or "Washington Flap" by UFO researchers and historians.

The once-secret Air Force documents prove that out.

The incident of the Kirksville, Missouri, radar sightings on July 12, 1952, was among about 200 from that year of the real-life UFO X-files contained in **Project Blue Book**.

Blue Book's case files are stored away at the National Archives in Washington, D.C.

If you've ever gone there, you'll have found you can't just walk in and have a look at the files as a tourist. You need to schedule an appointment just to even get into the material.

And much of what you can see there has been redacted — most of the names of witnesses were blotted out before the files were removed from their original resting place, which was Maxwell Air Force Base in Montgomery, Alabama.

However, there are some non-redacted copies available.

Before the redacted files were handed over to the National Archives, some early UFO research organizations made their own copies from the original Maxwell AFB documents.

The NICAP organization gets credit for obtaining the Maxwell versions and making them available for study on its website.

Fourteen more cases

As I began looking into the Kirksville radar case, I noticed there were 14 other UFO sightings in **Blue Book's** files around that same time period, from July 12 through July 14, 1952.

Here are the sightings, both identified and unidentified, and how **Blue Book** analyzed them (some of the documents are missing):

• **July 13 cases**: Southwest Washington D.C., evaluated as a meteor (cards missing); Kirksville, Missouri, (the radar case in this chapter) unidentified; Dayton, Ohio, meteor (cards missing); New Braintree, Massachusetts, balloon; Fordland, Missouri, insufficient data; Spokane, Washington, balloon; Dallas, Texas, insufficient data; Osceola, Wisconsin, radar interference (cards missing); Nevasseur AFB, Morocco, meteor, and Buffalo, New York, astronomical.

• **July 14 cases**: Norfolk, Virginia, unidentified; Washington, D.C., balloon; Great Falls AFB, Montana, insufficient data; Ryuku Islands (near Okinawa), insufficient data; Holloman AFB, New Mexico, balloon; and Oberlin Gardens, Pennsylvania, balloon (July 14 and 15).

While most were "identified," you have to remember that the Air Force was in the business of finding answers — they were out to assure the nation they were in charge of our air space. And if they could find a possible explanation, they would explain it — as long as the official explanation did NOT mention extraterrestrials.

Reading the blips

The Kirksville case contains no photos of the actual UFOs themselves, but it does have photos of their radar images on the radar screens.

The **Blue Book** files contain seven 5- by 7-inch black and white photographs of the live radar screens, which show the blips in different positions as they moved across the screen on every other sweep of the dial.

To most of us, these little white blobs on the screen don't tell us much.

But to the people who are trained to read the tiny nuances "painted" on the radar screens, the meaning of the sizes, shapes and the speeds of the blips in front of them was as clear as the words you're reading on this page.

And those blips were like nothing they had ever seen.

I found several documents associated with the Kirksville sighting, which are unembellished, unemotional descriptions of what the people working at those screens saw that night.

The first, is a short typed memo about the sighting:

"*At 0300Z on 13 Jul 52* [that would have been 9 p.m. Central Time on July 12], *the 790th AC/W Sq.* [Aircraft Control and Warning Squadron] *picked up an unidentified object traveling SE at a speed of 1,500 knots.*

"*The object was observed by controllers, electronic officers and the operator crew of this squadron with experience ranging from 1 to 5 years.*

"*Object painted on every other sweep of the radar. Standard electronics equipment was used. The blip presentation was the same as that of a B-36 or a B-50. No known air traffic in the vicinity. Thunderheads moving SE in area.*"

So what did the **Blue Book** analysts say about the sighting?

Strangely, one analyst blamed the weather. However, the blip was "*moving at a speed of 1,500 knots*" — I've never seen a cloud move that fast.

Six, not one, blips

The news reports and other written material on the Kirksville case seem to refer only to this one particular document, which wrongly indicates they saw only one blip — the other documents and photos in the old case file make it clear there were six different blips.

I'm not sure if that first memo was the only one released to the media at the time, or if the other documents were marked "classified" for a certain period.

So I might have a scoop — this might be the first time any journalist or researcher has reported there was NOT merely one object, but half a dozen UFOs possibly invading Missouri on the night of July 12, 1952.

About a dozen witnesses

Another document in the case file is a three-page electronic transmission that describes the movements of the six objects seen on the radar screens at Kirksville.

It cites specific points where they were first seen, how they moved and also says the speed of two of them was clocked as high as 4,800 mph.

It says the sightings were "witnessed by two operations crews, three controllers, three electronics officers, and two maintenance crews. Experience levels one to five years."

What about the weather?

"Unknown. Some cloud returns to west and northwest." That gives an entirely different picture of the weather than the first document.

That second document also said Kirksville had no air traffic in the vicinity of the blips.

The analysts at the **Blue Book** offices at Wright Patterson AFB in Dayton, Ohio, were apparently intrigued.

The analysts sent the commanding officer at Kirksville eight copies of radar data forms for the airmen working at the screens to fill out. The witnesses who saw the objects were ordered to fill out certified statements on July 17, 1952.

'Scope dopes' fill out reports

Filling out such a report about flying saucers might seem intimidating. But the witnesses stuck to their stories. I learned from the veteran-run **radomes.org** website that the radar operators called themselves "scope dopes."

The first report in the **Blue Book** files was from one of the scope dopes on duty that night, A/2C Robert W. Larson. Larson tracked three of the UFOs, or "Targets," and wrote certified statements for each of them.

On his first statement, titled "Target I," Larson lists the time as 0300Z on July 13.

The "Z" indicates worldwide Zulu Military Time used by aviation, so the time in their location in Missouri would have been six hours ahead, or 9 p.m. local time, on July 12.

Larson tracked the unidentified "Target 1" on the "PPI [Plan Position Indicator] scope No. 2."

His PPI scope No. 2 radar screen had a series of concentric circles. The center of the screen represented the antenna outside the building.

Giant golf ball

I found a description of the equipment used at the time on the **radome.org** website. The parabolic radar antenna was 42 feet wide and 22 feet tall. The massive antenna turned in a circle within what was called a radome, a 57.5-foot protective fiberglas sphere that looked a lot like a giant white golf ball.

The antenna operated in the S band with a frequency of 2,000 to 4,000 MHz.

The Kirksville installation was among 13 such radars in the permanent network of radar stations set up to defend the country against an aerial attack from Russia that might come in from the Arctic over Canada.

Kirksville's 54-acre base was built to fill in a radar gap that existed between Kansas City and Des Moines. Manufactured by the MIT Rad Lab, the AN/FPS-10 antenna had a 200-mile range, according to the **radomes.org** website.

As the radar antenna rotated clockwise, the screen showed the distance and position of the objects, which appear as white blobs, or "blips." Radar operators were trained to recognize the blips as corresponding to particular types of aircraft.

The blips "painted" or lingered on the screen until the antenna made another pass. If the blip moved to a new position, the radar crew could calculate its speed and direction.

Traveling 1,440–1,500 mph

Watching the radar, Larson was intrigued by the strange-looking blip he was seeing, which "continued to paint every other sweep. It seemed to move about 12 to 13 miles every time it appeared."

Based on its movement, Larson calculated the speed of "Target I" at 1,440 mph.

On another statement, titled "Target II," Larson said he tracked a second blip 15 minutes later, or 0315Z (9:15 p.m. CT) on PPI scope No. 2. Larson said Target II was moving at an estimated speed of 1,500 mph.

In a third certified statement, Larson says he tracked another blip, labeled "Target IV," starting at 0340Z (9:40 p.m. CT July 12) on PPI scope No. 2. Larson says Target IV moved 12 to 15 miles every other sweep, or about 1,500 mph.

"This target painted extremely large, about the size of a B-29," he wrote.

Could what he saw have been a B-29— maybe one on secret mission of some sort?

No, according to Boeing's technical specifications of the B-29 Superfortress.

It had a wingspan of 141 feet 3 inches and was 99 feet long. It was also loud, with four 2,200-horsepower engines.

And it had a cruising speed of 220 mph and a top speed of 365 mph — far too slow to match the speed of whatever was quietly zipping across Iowa and Missouri that night.

One hits speed of 1,640 mph

Next in the file were four certified statements from another "scope dope," A/3C Glenn R. Martin, who followed four of the objects on a different radar screen.

In his first statement, Martin says he also saw "Target I" on "PPI scope No. 6," at 0300Z (9 p.m. CT).

The unidentified target, Martin said, painted (formed an image on the screen) on every other sweep.

Target I appeared to move 11 to 15 miles on each sweep. The sweeps were operating at 4 RPMs (revolutions per minute).

In his statement, Martin indicated another Air Force command that went by the code name of "Prevail" was aware of the UFO — possibly from another radar antenna. Martin wrote: *"Prevail called us to inquire if we had a target in that area. When we picked it up we called back and notified Prevail. The estimated speed on this target was 1,440 mph."*

On a second certified statement, Martin said that at 0315Z (9:15 p.m. CT), he tracked "Target II" on PPI scope No. 6. He estimated its speed at 1,500 mph.

In a third statement, Martin said he tracked "Target III" on PPI scope No. 6 at 0320Z (9:20 p.m. CT). Martin said Target III always appeared to move 11 to 15 miles every two sweeps and they were operating at 4 RPMs. Martin estimated the speed of Target III at 1,640 mph.

Martin made a fourth certified statement that he saw "Target IV" at 0340Z (9:40 p.m. CT) on PPI scope No. 6. On every other sweep of the scope, it moved 12 to 15 miles. The estimated speed was 1,500 mph.

Targets travelled in straight line

Next in the case file were certified statements from another scope dope, A/3C Carl Van Laaten.

Van Laaten said at 0305Z (9:05 p.m.) while watching on PPI scope No. 2, he tracked "Target II," which moved 12 to 14 miles on every other sweep.

He referred to it as "track #32." The first position was at 001 degree at 151 miles and every other sweep it moved 12 to 14 miles. It stayed on the same heading, varying only about 1 or 2 degrees, he said. The last reading was at 354 degrees at 245 miles.

He wrote *"The target was called into Origin,"* which was apparently their command post. The speed was estimated at 1,500 mph.

In another statement, Van Laaten writes about tracking "Target III," at 0321Z (9:21 p.m.) on PPI scope No. 2.

Target III appeared every other sweep and went 14-16 miles each time it appeared on the screen. He calculated its speed at 1,640 p.m.

In a third statement by Van Laaten, he says he tracked another UFO, or "Target IV," at 0340Z (9:40 p.m. CT). He said it appeared on the screen at 321 degrees at 111 miles. On every other sweep it would appear in a new position, moving 12-15 miles, varying only 1 or 2 degrees on its heading. The last reading was at 320 degrees at 219 miles.

He estimated Target IV's speed at 1,500 mph.

UFOs the size of a B-29 or larger

The next statement in the files came from a fourth scope dope, A/1C Ray H. Foote, who also wrote about "Target I." Foote saw and tracked that "unidentified object" at 0300Z (9 p.m. CT) on PPI scope No. 2.

The blip first appeared at 142 degrees and 108 miles from the antenna. Foote said that target painted on the screen only on every other sweep and moved 12 miles every time it appeared. The target left the scope at 134 degrees at 234 miles after they tracked it for four minutes. The speed was estimated at 1,440 mph.

In a second certified statement, Foote wrote about watching "Target III." Foote said that at 320Z (9:20 p.m.), he picked up and tracked that unidentified object on PPI scope No. 2, traveling at a very fast speed.

Target III appeared first at 320 degrees azimuth and 128 miles away. It traveled at an estimated speed of 1,600 mph and appeared *about the size of a B-29 or larger.*

Foote wrote they could not obtain a height on Target III. It started at a position of 211 degrees and did not diminish in size until it left the scopes at 202 degrees azimuth and a range of 255 miles. He said the "Target III" blip was *of the normal shape of an aircraft, but very large and bright.* There was no weather showing in the area near the target, Foote wrote.

Two UFOs clocked at 4,800 mph

Another certified statement was from a fifth scope dope, A/2C Dwaine O. Johnson, also about "Target I." Johnson said at 0300Z (9 p.m. July 12, 1952) he witnessed and tracked an unidentified target picked up at 142 degrees and 108 miles.

Johnson said Target I showed up on the screen on every other sweep of the antenna and moved 12 to 13 miles each time.

"This target was called into us by Prevail and we picked it up immediately. It appeared in the size of a B-29. The estimated speed was 1,500 mph," Johnson wrote.

Two hours later, Johnson also tracked two more UFOs — and reported they were going three times faster than the first four objects.

In Johnson's certified statement, "Target V" appeared at 0504Z (11:04 p.m. CT on July 12), at 004 degrees at a range of 143 miles.

Target V appeared every sweep of the antenna and moved 20 miles each time.

"This target appeared in the size of a B-29 and kept at the same degrees until it was last seen. In this sector there was no unusual weather conditions or cloud formations. The last appearance of this target was at 004 degrees at 222 miles. I called into Orgin [sic] at soon as it appeared. The estimated speed was 4,800 mph."

Johnson's next certified statement was about "Target VI," which came into view three minutes later.

He wrote that he picked up Target VI on his scope at 004 degrees at 152 miles. It appeared every sweep of the antenna and moved 20 miles each time.

"This target appeared in the size of a B-29 and kept the same degrees until its last appearance. This target was called into Origin at its first appearance."

He said there were no cloud formations or unusual weather in the area. The last appearance of Target VI on his scope was at 004 degrees at 212 miles. The estimated speed was 4,800 mph.

Officer puzzled by 'unknown object'

One of the controllers on duty was 2nd Lt. Thomas Hogge, AO 842955, who wrote in a certified statement he did see an *"unknown object"* on the radar screen.

Like the other technicians, Hogge's statement shows his puzzlement.

"We were not able to obtain much information because the object appeared such a very short time and traveling at great speeds. The Blip presentation was approximately the same as that of a very large aircraft.

"Photographs were taken on the Plan Position Indicator. The flight characteristics was [sic] *not the same of any type aircraft that I am familiar with. I was unable to get any identification of the object."*

What were they?

Unfortunately, we don't know what happened after the analysts got the certified statements back from all the witnesses.

The case just seemed to end with a shrug — and was labeled as an "unknown."

Given that there were so many sightings in 1952, maybe it was just a manpower problem, possibly that **Blue Book's** investigators were already tapped out looking into other cases.

Or did the analysts know what they were? Could they have been a grouping of secret aircraft being tested by the military?

Also, why were none of our own aircraft scrambled to go see what they were? That seems very suspicious. And the fact that the news media was at first told there was only one object, not six, seems strange. Could this have been a prelude for what happened the next week in Washington, D.C.?

Unfortunately, we have no documents to check that out.

A CIA psy-ops test?

However, what we do have are speculations by UFO researchers from that time period and later that the government was hiding what it knew. It did so by classifying information as secret and by the CIA spreading disinformation.

In his book, *The Hynek UFO Report*, J. Allen Hynek, who worked as an analyst for **Project Blue Book**, says that the Air Force, in a report classified as "Secret" dated March 9, 1950, ordered all radar installations to report scope sightings of unusual objects.

Hynek says that because of the vagaries of radar propagation, radar sightings are the least reliable, although there are many cases that can't be easily dismissed.

The most reliable cases were those that also included visual sightings, he said.

However, the mindset was to explain away, rather than consider an extraterrestrial origin, he said.

*"Since **Project Blue Book** operated on the theory that there couldn't be any such thing as 'real' UFOs, the Air Force searched for almost any possible reason to explain away radar cases,"* Hynek wrote.

One of the military's top critics was Donald Keyhoe, a retired Marine major.

Keyhoe began questioning the military's investigations of UFOs and publishing what he uncovered. In his 1952 story in "True" Magazine, Keyhoe made a reference to the Kirksville case.

What Keyhoe wrote shows that he didn't have complete access to the **Project Blue Book** case files at the time — he thought only one UFO was seen:

*"**It was 9 p.m.** when Air Force radar men picked up an unknown object, its blip indicating a solid device or machine the size of a B-36. Before it raced off into the night, its speed was tracked at 1,500 knots — over 1,700 m.p.h.*

"Searching for a solution, one officer theorized that a thunderstorm might have caused the blip, but Washington Center controllers say this is impossible. To date, the A.T.I.C. [Air Technical Intelligence Center at Wright Patterson Air Force Base in Dayton, Ohio] has found no explanation."

(A B-36 was larger than a B-29. The B-36 had a wingspan of 230 feet, a length of 161 feet and was 46 feet tall. Interesting that the *official* story Keyhoe got was different than what the radar observers put in their certified statements.)

In another article for "True," published in 1967, Keyhoe noted there had been *"more than 300 cases of radar tracking and visual sightings confirmed by radar. In the ensuing years, there have been at least 2,000 additional radar cases in the U.S. alone. Reports have come from expert operators in the Army, Navy, Air Force, Marine Corps, Coast Guard, the Federal Aviation Agency (formerly the CAA) and pilots or radar operators of almost all the major airlines. The same situation exists in foreign countries.*

"Not only has radar proved UFO reality, it has accurately recorded the high UFO speeds, intricate maneuvers, precise UFO formations – including changes from one formation to another-and other important data which make it possible to evaluate UFO operations and help in the search for propulsion secrets."

Was Keyhoe correct? Or was somebody deliberately spoofing the data?

Could the CIA or another agency have been testing some fancy electronic equipment to produce false returns on radar screens in order to create the illusion of UFOs and possibly hide secret tests of spy planes, such as the U-2?

Keyhoe might not have known the technology to create ghost images on radar was being secretly developed at the time.

Spooky equation

But others were questioning radar data. In a 1962 article, *"ECM + CIA = UFO, or How to Cause a Radar Sighting,"* that possibility was posed by private UFO investigator Leon Davidson.

Davidson, a nationally known chemist and a member of the Manhattan Project, pointed out that as early as 1945, our military's planes began finding ways to trick radar by dropping aluminum foil strips and mechanically cluttering enemy radar screens.

Davidson says that by 1950, those foil strips were secretly being replaced by "electronic counter measures," or ECM, that were standard equipment in our bombers that could produce false readings on enemy radar screens.

In his article, Davidson quoted from a story in the March 1957 issue of *Aviation Research and Development* — an article that made me take notice that the six UFOs spotted on the Kirksville radar scopes could have been faked by the CIA.

"A new radar moving target simulator system — which generates a display of up to 6 individual targets on any standard radar indicator — has been developed . . . to train radar operators . . . and for in-flight testing of airborne early-warning personnel . . ."

Davidson writes: *"The reader should keep this quotation in mind when reading about radar sightings of high-speed UFOs."*

Psychological warfare

But why would the CIA try to trick our own radar operators?

Davidson explains: the *"mission of the CIA included waging psychological warfare."*

And he explained the meaning of his equation: *"I contend that since 1951, the CIA has caused or sponsored saucer sightings for its own purposes. By shrewd psychological manipulation, a series of 'normal' events has served up so as to appear as quite convincing evidence of extraterrestrial UFOs."*

Davidson theorized that ECM techniques were responsible for the famous Washington, D.C., National Airport sightings on July 19 and 26, 1952.

In those sightings, perhaps the most famous of the 1952 flying saucer sightings, seven blips were seen flying 15 miles south-southwest of the nation's capital on radar.

More objects were seen on radar flying over the White House and the Capitol. An orange object was spotted visually in the sky.

Jet fighters were scrambled to intercept them, but the objects mysteriously disappeared. Then they reappeared after the jets left.

The blips reappeared on the following Saturday, July 27, with both visual and radar sightings reported.

The two weekends of radar sightings over the Capitol had the effect of scaring people and generating headlines across the country. The Air Force had to hold a press conference to assure the news media that it was in control of the nation's skies.

Davidson notes the ECM was a classified subject at that time, so they weren't even considered at the time as possible explanations.

The Air Force blamed the sightings on temperature inversions, which officials claimed played tricks on radar screens — an explanation that has since been roundly criticized by many researchers. The visual sightings were dismissed as meteors or misidentified stars or planets.

But were those the real causes?

Could Davidson be right? Were the UFOs seen on radars across the country during 1952 a CIA test of electronic counter measures— not only to see if they could simulate UFOs, but see how people, such as radar operators, reacted to them psychologically?

Or were these real flying saucers from outer space?

To this day, we still don't know for sure.

But the sightings continue, despite the Air Force's formal investigation being over.

Modern-day radar sightings

In researching radar sightings, I ran across a June 2016 story carried on a few news websites about a Canadian UFO researcher, Victor Viggiani, who received enlightening information— the North American Aerospace Defense Command (NORAD) has confirmed it tracks *an average of 1,800 UFOs a year* on radar.

At a UFO conference in Canada, Viggiani released a document that says, *"The NORAD commander has approved the release of the following information regarding Tracks Of Interest and unknown tracks.*

"The yearly average in the past five years has been 1,800 TOIs and 75 intercepts."

Intercepts? Yes, that says 75 intercepts.

Viggiani's persistence in tracking down a paper trail of radar-inspired NORAD jet fighter chases through a Canadian Access to Information Act request shows that the military has gone after UFOs 1,800 times a year and has made contact with them 75 times each year.

However, those two numbers were all that Viggiani could shake out of the secrecy tree — nothing about how many were earthly objects or if any were extraterrestrial in nature.

As of this writing, you could find out more about Viggiani's findings on the website **ZlandCommunicationsNewsNetwork.blogspot.com.**

Secret tracking for decades

The website says the documents show the U.S. and Canada have had a secret system in place to track and chase UFOs for decades and have kept what they've found from the public.

"This lack of transparency surrounding a national security issue suggests that either Canadian government officials are totally ignorant of the facts surrounding the UFO matter — or they and the infrastructure of government and its military have something to hide with respect to the existence of UFOs," according to the website.

Meanwhile, I've continued to delve into the early sightings cases.

In the next chapter, I look at another one reported in July 1952. But this one was a visual sighting in Kansas City — and it's also an "X File," listed among the 701 "unknown" in **Project Blue Book**.

2. Green UFO over KC

KANSAS CITY, Missouri (July 26, 1952) — It was the kind of thing that would startle you — particularly when flying saucers had just been all over the news.

A military officer's wife who had been stargazing was the first to spot it.

She had been looking out at the night sky, just after midnight, in her home in Kansas City, Missouri.

The object had an emerald greenish color. It was moving slowly across the sky. Red-orange flashes emanated from it. She alerted her husband, a U.S. Air Force captain. Together, they kept track of it for an hour. Others working in the control towers of two nearby airports also saw it.

It's easy to imagine what they were all thinking as they watched this green goblin over Kansas City.

Was it one of our own aircraft — perhaps some secret technology being tested? Could it belong to the Russians? Were we under attack?

Or was it a strange being from another world that was hovering over the earth, a craft like many others that had been reported around the country in the past month, including several the previous weekends flying over Washington, D.C.?

As of this writing, almost 66 years have passed since the unidentified object over Kansas City was seen. And not one plausible explanation has emerged as to what it was.

The Kansas City sighting is still listed in the archives of the Air Force's **Project Blue Book** as an "unknown," one of the government's once classified early X-files.

Meager documentation

This cold case sighting is one of the more interesting Missouri unsolved **Project Blue Book** files that were once secret and marked as "unknown," but have since become unclassified.

The only details of the sighting I could find were contained in seven pages in the **Project Blue Book** files.

The first document in the file is Air Force Form 112, Part I, an Air Intelligence Information Report, with the subject "Unidentified Flying Object (FLYOBRT)," which appears to be mainly a reference card for the sighting.

Capt. Roy A. Lancaster, an Air Force intelligence officer, prepared the report from information he received over the phone.

Lancaster's summary says that *"On 26 July 1952, at approximately 0015 hours, Captain Harry A. Stone, AO 791157, Air Force Installation Representative, Kansas City Area Engineers, observed an airborne object over Kansas City, Missouri."*

On the next page, we learn that Stone immediately telephoned the dispatcher at Fairfax Field, an Air Force installation just west across the Missouri River north of Kansas City, Kansas.

"The dispatcher subsequently notified the tower operators of the Fairfax and Municipal Airports of the incident, who also saw the object," Lancaster writes.

Lancaster also made reference to "paragraph 7c, AFL 200-5," which was Air Force Chief of Staff Hoyt S. Vandenberg's directive from April 29, 1952, on how to gather UFO information — information that was to be kept secret from the public.

Under that document, UFO reports were to include the code "FLYOBRPT" in the heading to make it easier to identify in "electrical," or teletype, transmissions.

At minimum, the report had to be classified as "restricted." And *"Local publicity concerning this reporting and analysis activity is to be avoided."*

In his report about the Kansas City sighting, Lancaster wrote there was a single object, apparently round in shape, of an unknown size.

It was *"predominantly greenish with intermittent red orange flashes shooting from edge in all directions."*

He notes the UFO was seen at 12:15 a.m. and was kept under observation until about 1:15 a.m.

His report covered the required information for reporting UFOs.

For example, the observers used binoculars to kept it in sight. The weather was clear and there were slight winds at the time. No photos were taken. There were no aircraft around or meteorological conditions that might have accounted for the sighting.

And they must not have felt too threatened — there were no attempts to intercept the UFO to identify it, the report said.

Witness details sighting

As in most UFO case reports I've researched, the best information came from the written narrative submitted by the observer.

The third document in the case file has what Stone and his wife saw from their new two-bedroom home at 4006 Vineyard Road in Kansas City, Missouri.

A modern-day real estate website says the house was built that same year of the sighting. So I could picture the couple possibly sitting out in their new backyard, looking to the west, cooling off on a warm July Friday night.

The Stones might have even been looking for UFOs. According to Capt. Edward Ruppelt, then the head of **Project Blue Book**, 40 reports a day were coming to his attention that month. Many people were turning out to look at the skies, probably as a result of all the UFO newspaper and magazine reports from that year.

"At approximately 15 minutes past midnight my wife called my attention to what appeared to be an unusually bright star in the western sky," Stone writes.

"I observed this object through binoculars for about 10 minutes and then notified the dispatcher at Fairfax Field, Kansas, of what I was looking at and it's [sic] location. I continued to keep the object under observation with the binoculars until approximately 15 minutes past one o'clock A.M. At this time it had apparently sunk so low on the horizon I could no longer keep it in view."

Stone's formal report continued with a checklist he made:

• First observed: 0015 26 July 52.

• Location: WNW from observer at angle of about 40 degrees from horizontal.

• Shape: Indeterminate, appeared to be round more than anything else.

• Size: Unknown, but gave the impression of being quite large.

• Altitude: Unknown, but based on intensity of lights would estimate 35,000 to 40,000 feet.

• Speed: Took about one hour to cover 30 degrees of arc in the sky.

• Course: Appeared to travel in a northwesterly direction, with no apparent loss of altitude or change in speed.

• Last observed: 0115 26 July 52, WNW from observer at an angle of about 10 degrees from the horizontal.

Not a 'conventional aircraft'

Stone then listed his general impressions:

• Only lights were observed, no substance was determined.

• Not believed to be any type of conventional aircraft.

• Weather was clear, no lighting in area.

• Wish to emphasize that estimates of size and altitude given above are unreliable due to lack of adequate data on which to accurately judge. They are purely guestimates.

Stone also wrote that during the entire time he watched the object, he could detect no sound coming from it.

Stone also included two sketches of his home and the direction the object travelled.

The sketches were neatly drawn and labeled, giving the impression Stone was very serious about what he saw. He apparently took no photos.

Electrical report filed

The file also had an "electrical" report (teletype) in all capital letters with abbreviated words that was sent out from Fairfax Field that night to offices that included the Air Technical Intelligence Headquarters in Washington, D.C., and ATIC at Wright Patterson AFB in Dayton, Ohio. The first line mentioned "FLYOBRPT," meaning it was pertaining to UFOs. (The report had many abbreviated words.)

"EXTREMELY LARGE OBJ PRIMARILY EMERALD GREEN ... WITH FREQUENT RED FLASHES FR THE CIRCUM ... NO DISCERNABLE AERODYNAMIC FEATURES OR TRAIL OF EXHAUST ...

PRPLN SYS (PROPULSION SYSTEM) NOT IDENTIFIED ... EXTREMELY SLOW ... NO AUDIBLE SOUND ...MUD IN UNDULATING SIDE TO SIDE MANNER DISAPPEARED OVER THE HORIZON (HAD HOURS SEEN) ... USING SIX BY 30 CANADIAN BINOCULARS ... ALTITUDE 35,000-40,000 FEET. APPROXIMATELY 18 MILES DIS."

The electrical transmission also said Stone saw it first and that it was further observed by "CAA tower operators." It said there was no reported meteorological activity and they obtained no physical evidence. "No interception action taken. No reported aircraft in area of sighting."

Why didn't they send up a plane?

What can we make of the sighting in hindsight?

Not only was the sighting strange, but the military's reaction to it seemed even stranger, given that UFO reports were coming in from all over the country and the Air Force was under pressure to explain them.

Capt. Stone took great care in immediately notifying authorities at Fairfax. He took great care in recording his observations. He even submitted detailed drawings.

The fact that it was also seen by observers in two other locations — not just citizens, but airport tower operators trained to identify all kinds of aircraft — would have seemed to have added to the urgency of a response.

The tower operators had ruled out other aircraft. They had ruled out balloons. There was no strange weather.

The UFO didn't appear to be moving that fast. So why didn't they send up a plane to check it out?

We don't know because the **Blue Book Report** doesn't have any information from those tower operators.

Weren't they also interviewed? Where are their statements? Who made the decision not to send up a plane to find out what the object was?

Or does the **Project Blue Book** report give us only part of that report?

Men in Black

Over the years, many independent UFO researchers believe there were other agencies that were conducting their own classified investigations separate from **Project Blue Book**, including the CIA and the NSA.

We do know that there was a hush-hush unit, the 4602d Air Intelligence Service Squadron, which became the lead investigator as early as 1952 for the more promising **Blue Book** cases.

The 4602d had been put together to recover any crashed enemy aircraft in any weather and in any terrain.

The crash debris was to be taken to Wright Patterson AFB in Dayton, Ohio, where it would be analyzed and reverse engineered to learn any secrets from foreign technology.

As part of its clandestine directive, the 4602d also came to be charged with investigating UFOs in the "Zone of the Interior," or the 48 contiguous U.S. states. (The 5004th AISS did the same in Alaska.)

The smallest operational unit of the 4602d was the Combat Intelligence Team, which consisted of one officer or noncommissioned officer and two airmen.

Some UFO researchers have guessed these three-man teams were the mysterious "men in black" who often showed up after UFO sightings to question witnesses — and sometimes warn them to forget what they had seen.

CUFON (Computer UFO Network), an organization that has been collecting UFO-related government documents since 1983, has a formerly secret report on its website about the history of the 4602d.

The report indicates that by 1954, the 4602d was conducting follow-up UFO field investigations for ATIC and that during 1954 it had resolved 77 of 124 cases it studied, with only 35 cases unresolved.

In looking at the Kansas City green UFO report, it made me wonder whether the 4602d — or the CIA or NSA — was brought in for the Kansas City investigation.

That would make more sense than just dropping the case as an unknown. But that raises even more questions.

If the "men in black" did follow through with a field investigation, what did they learn? Did they talk to anyone else who might have seen the green UFO on that warm July night in 1952?

Are their detailed reports still hidden away after 64 years in the compartmentalized "need to know" labyrinth of military bureaucracy? Why?

In Chapter 3, I'll take a look at an "unknown" cold case that was possibly checked out by the "men in black" from the 4602d.

It features another green object seen over Missouri — this one two summers later in 1954.

PART 2:

THE WAVE OF 1954

By 1954, Project Blue Book was recording hundreds of sightings a year. However, the Air Force seemed to be no closer to finding out what UFOs were. A look through the documents shows investigations seemed to downplayed and routinely placed in files marked "unknown" or "unexplained."

However, the public was still reporting the strange lights they were seeing in the sky — enough that UFO researchers regard them as the "Wave of 1954."

Chapters 3, 4 and 5 in this book are sightings from Missouri that to this day are still unexplained — and can be considered part of the Air Force's real-life X-Files.

3. Lights over St. Louis

NORMANDY, Missouri, (July 18, 1954) — It's unlikely the two St. Louis area men had ever met or knew they had something in common.

Sixty-two years ago as of this writing, on a warm clear July evening, viewing from different positions in the greater St. Louis metropolitan area, both men saw something unusual in the night sky.

Thomas Chamblin saw his puzzling object from his home in the St. Louis suburb of Normandy, Missouri. The time was 8:40 p.m.

Five minutes later, across the Mississippi River, about 17 miles to the southwest in East St. Louis, Illinois, Anthony J. Zillen saw something similar.

Could they have been the same UFO?

Each man saw a large, bright disc-shaped object. Each described an object that didn't behave like a plane, a balloon or a meteor. It was something that didn't look like anything either man had seen before.

What they saw seemed so unusual that both men, each a military veteran, felt compelled to contact the U.S. Air Force, which was the main government agency assigned to investigate such sightings.

It may have been out of a sense of duty, just in case it might be an invading Russian missile or jet — at the time, the U.S. and the Soviet Union were in the midst of the Cold War.

Or maybe Chamblin and Zillen were each hoping to find out if what they saw was one of those mysterious flying saucers that were suddenly being reported all over the country.

But what exactly each saw is still a mystery. It's a mystery made even more complex by the way the Air Force has catalogued the two sightings.

Both cases are among the thousands of UFO reports, most of them once classified, that are part of the Air Force's aging *Project Blue Book* files.

But let me back up.

Zillen's sighting over East St. Louis was actually put into the "explained" category. Some intelligence officer or analyst explained it away as a "probable aircraft."

In contrast, Chamblin's sighting, at roughly the same time and place, was put into the "unknown" bin — it's still one of **Project Blue Book's** unexplained cold cases, a case I like to call a real-life X-file.

Why were the two sightings not linked? Who investigated each one?

These are questions that are difficult to explain, given the secrecy at the time surrounding the Air Force's investigation of UFOs and that many ufologists now believe that **Project Blue Book** wasn't the only government program dealing with UFOs.

Although **Blue Book** was shut down in 1969, Freedom of Information requests by UFO researchers indicate that other agencies, including the FBI and CIA, were — and probably still are — looking into UFO sightings around the world.

I came across the two St. Louis sightings, and the fact that they happened at roughly the same time in the same place, as I was looking into some of the "unidentified" cases from Missouri.

Chamblin's sighting has been catalogued by other UFO researchers as one of the 701 "unidentified" sightings or "unknowns" in **Project Blue Book**. Non-government researchers find they're the more interesting cases because they could be either a secret U.S. or foreign technology — or an extraterrestrial technology.

Most of the information I found about each case from previous researchers didn't go into much detail on what Chamblin saw. So I decided to check out the once-classified original documents to see if I could learn more details.

Little documentation

The first item in **Project Blue Book's** Chamblin case file is a Project 10073 Record Card, or ATIC Form 329, a standardized index card used to summarize a UFO case's basic details.

The Chamblin report says the incident occurred on July 18, 1954, with the Greenwich Mean Time, or Zulu time, listed as "19/0240Z," or 8:40 p.m. local time.

The record card also says Chamblin's sighting was a "Ground-Visual" observation, that there were no photos taken and the source was a "Civilian."

The length of the observation was 30 minutes, the number of objects seen was one, and its course was westerly.

Unfortunately, the summary has some abbreviation, misspellings and typos: *"Greenish white object at 30 deg elevation, 30 deg azimuth moving W. Dsiappear to NW in 30 minutes by fading from view winds from NW. Two reports F-86's in area. Ocassional lightening."*

In the Comments section, it says *"Object in sight for 30 minutes. Moving into wind."*

In the "Conclusions" area, there are 12 possible boxes on the record card that could be checked. The first three are *"Was Balloon," "Probably Balloon"* and *"Possibly Balloon,"* with the same three choices for *"Aircraft"* and *"Astronomical."*

The last three boxes of conclusions were the choices *"Other,"* with a space to write; *"Insufficient Data for Evaluation,"* and *"Unknown."*

The Chamblin sighting **Blue Book** record card shows two conclusions were reached: the *"Unknown"* box is checked. And, next to *"Other,"* the word *"UNIDENTIFIED"* is typed in all capital letters.

The only other document in the case file is a multipage "electrical" report typed in all capital letters.

Rather than going through the mail, such "electrical" documents were immediately transmitted over telephone lines to those in charge of making sure our airspace was secure.

They immediately went to the Director of Intelligence in Washington, D.C., the Commander of the Air Defense Command in Ent Air Force Base in Colorado Springs, Colorado, and the Commander of ATIC in Wright-Patterson AFB in Dayton, Ohio.

An answer sheet

At first glance, the document seems to be written in code, until you realize many words were abbreviated. Also, the transmission didn't make a lot of sense until I realized it was an answer sheet — I just needed to find out what questions were being asked.

Fortunately, I happened to find the questionnaire that the intelligence officers at Air Force bases were required to ask.

The standard questions were contained in a regulation known as Air Force Letter No. 200-2, dated April 29, 1952, which explained how to report unidentified flying objects, then called *UFOBs*.

UFOBs were defined as *"any airborne object which by performance, aerodynamic characteristics, or unusual features, does not conform to any presently known aircraft or missile type, or which cannot be positively identified as a familiar object."*

The regulation said the *"Air Force interest in unidentified flying objects is twofold: First as a possible threat to the security of the United States and its forces, and secondly, to determine technical aspects involved."*

Once I found the standard questions the commanders at the bases were required to ask, it was simple to plug in the answers from the "electrical" report on the Chamblin sighting.

Then I ran into another problem.

Unfortunately, the first page seemed to be partially missing from the **Project Blue Book** files I had located online. These were files that had been probably been handled several times by not only by **Project Blue Book** analysts, but in later years by UFO researchers who went to do research on them at Maxwell AFB in Alabama and by those who handled them at their final resting place in the National Archives in Washington D.C.

In other words, what I was looking at online were the remains of what were left in what might have been a bigger file.

However, I was able to match up the second page fairly well enough to get some more details about what Chamblin saw.

For example, we learn Chamblin's UFO was not only shaped like a disc, he said it was the size of a golf ball held in the hand at arm's length.

For comparison purposes, the full moon is about the size of a pea held at arm's length. Yes, that seems small. But you can try it for yourself. So unless Chamblin was exaggerating, the UFO must have loomed very large in the night sky.

He also described the color being *"greenish white."*

I learned from the electrical report that Chamblin couldn't make out any familiar features on the UFO, that it didn't have a trail of exhaust and he couldn't hear any sound coming from it.

What drew his attention to it?

The form says, *"Brilliance caught observers eye."*

Chamblin spotted the large greenish white disc from his home at 7329 Burwood Ave.

He watched that Sunday night in July as it traveled west for 30 minutes, then finally lost sight of it as it headed northwest. He estimated it being at an altitude of 20,000 feet.

Chamblin also said there was occasional lightning in the area. The electrical report also indicates he was asked if what he saw might have been something astronomical — a planet or a meteor.

Chamblin told the investigators no, but he did see something astronomical: *"Observer sighted shooting star at aprx same time, but claims it does not compare with object."*

We don't know anything from the report about Chamblin himself except that he was 28 years old, was a civilian, but had formerly been a private in the Army.

A 'star-like' object

There was a second sighting that night in the St. Louis area. The witness was Anthony Zillen, 8300 St. Philip Drive, East St. Louis, Ill.

Zillen, a 33-year-old civilian, was in the Navy Reserves, attached to the VA-924 Fighter Attack Squadron in St. Louis.

The Project 10073 Record Card summarizing Zillen's report said the East St. Louis man saw a *"star-like"* object for three to five minutes. It made steady movements to the south or southwest. It was shaped like a disc and was estimated to be at an altitude of 30,000 to 40,000 feet.

The **Project Blue Book** record card shows the investigator typed an X in a box on the form labeled *"Was Aircraft."* Below that it says *"Probable a/c (aircraft) Sighting."*

The Zillen sighting gives the time as GMT 19/0245Z, which was 8:45 p.m. on July 18 St. Louis time. As I noted earlier, that's only a five-minute difference from when Chamblin saw his brilliant greenish-white disc-like object 17 miles away.

The other document on Zillen's sighting indicates what he saw was comparatively large — or he was exaggerating its size.

The question form asks him how big it was compared to everyday objects held at arm's length.

Again, for comparison purposes, a full moon might seem large in the sky, but if you held your arm out, it would only be about the size of a pea held at arm's length.

Zillen says his disc-shaped glowing object was the size of a grapefruit — yes, a grapefruit — held at arm's length.

He described it as being "Yellowish Gold" in color and as bright as a star.

He explained he couldn't make out any other details, but it appeared to be just one object.

The object left no tail or trail of exhaust. It made no sound.

Asked what drew his attention to it, he explained it was the object's movement.

Could Zillen's UFO have been an aircraft, as the analyst concluded? Could Zillen have made a mistake?

That's questionable.

The information on Zillen says he was in the Navy Reserves in a fighter squadron based out of St. Louis. That means he had seen many planes flying at night. And what he saw the night of July 18, 1954 — a bright yellow-gold glowing object the size of a grapefruit held at arm's length — didn't match up to what he would have known was a plane flying at night.

But if it wasn't a plane, what was it?

Like Chambin, Zillen said the object he saw was at an elevation of about 30 degrees and an azimuth of 30 degrees.

However, it was traveling in the opposite direction as Chamblin's UFO — Chamblin's went west, then northwest over 30 minutes. Zillen's went south to southwest before he lost sight of it after five minutes.

Could there have been two similar UFOs flying over the St. Louis area that same evening?

Unfortunately, unlike some of the other **Project Blue Book** cases, neither of the two sightings has any other documentation.

A wave of sightings

What we do know about 1954 is that it was a big year for UFO sightings around the world.

NICAP (National Investigations Committee on Aerial Phenomena) refers to those sightings as the "Great Wave of 1954." NICAP's website has a 19-page report going through the cases on their website.

The report showed 63 cases were filed by **Project Blue Book** from all over the world in July, including the two St. Louis area cases. However, the Air Force's **Blue Book** analysts evaluated many of them as either having "insufficient data" or as being astronomical.

Why didn't the Air Force investigate further?

The official reason was that once they thought a sighting didn't represent a threat, they dropped it.

However, there were two formal studies done by outside agencies of the reports gathered by **Project Blue Book** and its predecessors.

One was the *Robertson Panel*, which was convened in 1953 after the public became worried about all of the visual and radar sightings over Washington D.C. and throughout the country in 1952 *(See Chapter 2).*

The panel, formed on a recommendation by the CIA's Office of Scientific Intelligence, was headed by H.P. Robertson, a cosmologist physicist of the California Institute of Technology, to look into the UFO reports that had been gathered up through November 1952.

The Robertson Panel met for only four days. And in that short amount of time concluded there was nothing in the reports that couldn't be explained by natural phenomena — a conclusion that many UFO researchers have criticized. Critics said the panel arrived at their decision too hastily with too much influence from the CIA.

The panel also reportedly suggested a public campaign to begin stripping UFOs of the *"special status they have been given and the aura of mystery they have unfortunately acquired"* — a suggestion some researchers think was guided by the CIA.

The panel's report — and the recommendations to begin a campaign to discredit UFO witnesses — was kept classified for 20 years. It was eventually obtained by UFO researchers through the Freedom of Information Act and made public.

The Robertson Panel's repercussions frustrated some scientists who worked for the government as consultants, including J. Allen Hynek.

Hynek, a professor of astronomy who worked in the early days of the Air Force UFO investigations to provide astronomical explanations for UFOs, later on had a change of heart when he saw how many could not being explained without further data.

He presented testimony to a congressional committee in 1968 to request a better, more scientific, study of UFOs than what the Air Force was doing.

In his testimony, Hynek said *"It is most logical to ask why do not the unidentified in the Air Force files call forth investigative efforts in depth and of wide scope. The answer is compound: the Air Force position is that there is no evidence that UFO's represent a threat to the national security: consequently it follows that it is not their mission to be scientifically curious about the hundreds of unidentified cases in their own files."*

At that same symposium, James McDonald, Senior Physicist, Institute of Atmospheric Physics, University of Arizona, also called for funding a scientific study.

McDonald told the Committee on Science and Astronautics, "*I emphasize that my experience is that again and again you find people who were not really interested in UFO's until they saw one themselves.*

"Then they suddenly became very, very concerned, as one more member of the public who has become a UFO witness; and in this body of citizens there are some very distressed persons who wish that the scientific community, or the Government, were doing something about this problem."

McDonald said the reason scientists haven't studied UFOs is because they have no hard evidence to study.

"The scientific community as a whole won't take this problem seriously because it doesn't have scientific data. They want instrumental data," he wrote in his testimony.

"Why don't they have instrumental data? Because the scientists don't take it seriously enough to get the scientific data. It is like the 20-year-old who can't get a job because he lacks experience, and he lacks experience because he hasn't had a job.

"In the same way you find the scientist wishing you would give him good hard meter readings and magnetometer traces, and so on: but we don't have it yet because the collective body of scientists, including myself, have ignored UFOs."

By the time the reports from Chamblin and Zillen were filed in 1954, the Air Force seemed to be in more of cataloging mode than a research mode on the sightings.

They seemed to be more interested in proving that UFOs were not a security threat than actually determining what they could be.

One of the interesting points that the scientists brought up at the 1968 symposium was that at one time meteors were seen in the same light as UFOs — as folklore.

Scientists initially dismissed the idea that rocks could actually be falling from space until they began formally and began systematically collecting and studying evidence.

Scientists like McDonald and Hynek wanted to go beyond the idea that people were merely mistaking explainable sights in the sky for something unusual or out of this world.

McDonald took it upon himself to personally interview witnesses involved in at least 300 UFO sightings. And after talking to them, he said he was open to the idea that UFOs could be machines that were being controlled by either some unknown government or even extraterrestrial entities.

Meanwhile, both Hynek and McDonald were also still open at the time that UFOs might represent some new phenomenon that we could not perceive because we hadn't been looking at UFOs in quite the right way. The Air Force was looking at them as a possible threat, not as an opportunity to gain new technology and learn more about the universe.

There was at least one scientist at the symposium who seemed to throw cold water — at least lukewarm water — on any further attempts to study UFOs — Carl Sagan.

Sagan at the time was an associate professor of astronomy at Cornell.

Sagan, who later went on to become the leading public voice toward studying the cosmos, basically told the congressional committee he didn't think a major scientific study of UFOs could be justified:

"... I believe it would be much better advised to support the biology, the Mariner, and Voyager programs of NASA, and the radio astronomy programs of the National Science Foundation, than to pour very much money into this study of UFOs.

"On the other hand, I think a moderate support of investigations of UFOs might very well have some scientific paydirt in it, but perhaps not the one that we are talking about today."

Unfortunately, more than six decades have passed since the two episodes over St. Louis in 1954. And nearly half a century has passed since the Air Force shut down **Project Blue Book** in 1969.

As with some of the other incidents I've recounted, it might be worthwhile to take another look at some of these UFO reports.

Hynek and McDonald, at that 1968 symposium, saw what happened when only one government agency was looking into the topic — it appeared very little study was done once the sighting was determined not to be an immediate threat.

They recommended to the congressional panel, quite emphatically, that more studies be funded and that they involve multiple agencies.

They recommended looking at the UFO phenomenon from different perspectives, similarly to what was being done at the time about solving the problems of disease and world hunger.

The Air Force was in the process of having an outside study of the UFO situation at the time of the symposium.

In 1967, the Air Force contracted with the University of Colorado, initially for $325,000, to complete a 12-month study of the photos, video, and witness interviews from the Air Force's own investigations.

That study, eventually known as the **Condon Report**, came out in 1969 with the verdict that "further extensive study of UFOs probably cannot be justified in the expectation that science will be advanced thereby."

The report also suggested that the Air Force could maintain its surveillance and defense functions without the need for a special unit, such as **Project Blue Book**.

They also disagreed that UFOs were being clouded in government secrecy — *"We have no evidence of secrecy concerning UFO reports. What has been miscalled secrecy has been no more than an intelligent policy of delay in releasing data so that the public does not become confused by premature publication of incomplete studies of reports."*

Unfortunately the Air Force never followed through on that recommendation — at least in the open. However, other agencies such as NICAP and MUFON continued with their own research.

In Chapter 4, we move on to another Missouri sighting during the *Great Wave of 1954.*

4. Butler's lights

BUTLER, Missouri, (Sept. 4, 1954) — You might be familiar with one of the classic cases of UFO lore, the sighting known as the "Lubbock Lights" in September 1951 in Lubbock, Texas.

That unexplained sighting of a string of U-shaped lights seen by three university professors was one of the earliest UFO observations to gain national publicity.

Or you might have heard of the more modern "Phoenix Lights" — the string of lights in a V-shaped pattern flying over Phoenix, Arizona, on the night of March 13, 1997. Thousands of people saw them, including Arizona's governor.

But did you know Butler, Missouri, had something similar?

According to the Air Force's **Project Blue Book** records, on Sept. 4, 1954 — about three years after the Lubbock Lights and about 43 years earlier than the Phoenix Lights— there were at least three people who saw a string of lights pass over Butler, a town about 50 miles south of Kansas City, not too far east of Missouri's border with Kansas.

A wave of sightings

The Butler lights were among dozens of UFO sightings that took place during 1954 in the U.S. They were also part of a cluster of sightings, what today's UFO researchers are calling the *"Wave of 1954"* that were reported throughout Europe that year.

Most of the European 1954 sightings were not part of the Air Force's **Project Blue Book** investigation. But someone in our government was checking them out.

UFO researchers for NICAP (**http://www.nicap.org/waves/-1954fullrep.htm**) report that formerly classified documents that have been made public through Freedom of Information Act requests reveal that the CIA had been translating and analyzing foreign newspaper and magazine clippings about the 1954 sightings.

What that shows clearly is there were two faces concerning our government's UFO studies.

One was the public face, which was designed to placate those who reported UFO and to assure the public there was nothing to worry about.

To the public, it seemed the military had only a mild, if begrudging, interest through the Air Force's **Project Blue Book** in tracking the sightings to make sure they were no security threat to U.S. airspace.

However, we now know there was a second, hidden face. The CIA was secretly researching those 1954 events. The CIA documents shows that those in the intelligence community were also highly interested on what was being reported around the world. Did they know what was going on?

A city of lights

But what about Butler? Its history had been shaped by the Civil War, having once been ravaged by Union forces in retaliation for the 1863 sacking of Lawrence, Kansas.

In rebuilding, Butler's citizens proved to be progressive — in 1881, it became the first city in Missouri and the first west of the Mississippi to bring in electric lighting.

 The city's website still labels it "The Electric City," showing an ornate courthouse surrounded by brick streets and historic homes.

Interestingly, Butler could also lay claim to an emerging beacon of light in the science fiction genre: Robert A. Heinlein.

Heinlein, who was born in Butler in 1907 and grew up in nearby Kansas City, had by 1954 just published *Starman Jones* (set in a future Ozarks Mountains) and would in 1961 publish his acclaimed *Stranger in a Strange Land*.

By 1954 Butler had around 3,500 people, according to census records.

One of them was a man whose name pops up in the Air Force **Project Blue Book** records: J. Faltemeier.

Faltemeier at the time was a 34-year-old airways operations specialist in communications for the Civil Aeronautics Administration (CAA), the precursor to today's Federal Aviation Administration (FAA).

The witness

Unfortunately, Faltemeier's name has been covered over or blotted out on the pages of the Butler report that are in the **Blue Book** archives located at the National Archive in Washington, D.C.

However, before those documents were transferred to the National Archives, they had been housed in their original format in Maxwell Air Force Base in Montgomery, Alabama, and had been available to UFO researchers for decades.

An early non-government organization that was studying the UFO phenomenon, the National Investigative Committee on Aerial Phenomena (NICAP) had gone through the original non-redacted **Blue Book** documents at Maxwell.

So it's because of NICAP's early research that we're able to learn Faltemeier's name and the names of many of the other witnesses in the other "unknowns" that would have been lost to history.

(Whenever names are redacted in the **Blue Book** files from the National Archives, I've tried to find out if their corresponding pages from the Maxwell files have been posted online somewhere.)

The sighting

Faltemeier's "unknown" sighting of the Butler lights is detailed on a **Project Blue Book** teletype "electrical" report, sent from the Lowry Flight Service Center in Denver, Colorado, to JEDEN/COMDR Air Defense Command at Ent Air Force Base, Colorado. It was also sent to the JEDWP/COMDR Air Technical Intelligence Center at Wright-Patterson, Dayton, Ohio.

The form was at first a little confusing for me to decipher. It contains numbers, letters, and what appeared to be answers. As I learned on an earlier report I tried to decipher, I realized the answers matched up to the questions on the standard form used at the time by the USAF's base commanders to report UFO sightings.

The summary card for the sighting provides basic details. It says that Faltemeier, who was apparently working overnight at the base airport, saw the strange sight at 3 a.m. on Sept. 4, 1954.

There is no narrative of his report, which would have been helpful and might have included his own words.

What we know from the condensed version is Faltemeier saw between 20 and 30 lights that appeared to be across from each other "as if on string" that flew straight and level for about 90 seconds.

But the responses to the questions posed on the Air Force's standard UFO reporting form provided a little more detail.

Asked in the questionnaire how large the objects were, Faltemeier reported that when he extended his arm, a finger would obscure the objects.

He said the lights were white. Although they appeared to be strung together, he couldn't tell if they were flying in a particular formation.

He couldn't make out any discernable features or details that would have identified them as aircraft. He also was not sure if the objects left a trail or any exhaust in their wake.

Unlike the roar of the aircraft engines of his day, the objects made no sound.

Asked what first called his attention to the objects, Faltemeier said he caught sight of the objects as he was taking a weather observation.

He was also asked to estimate the angle of elevation and the altitude. When he first saw them, the objects were overhead, between 30,000 and 50,000 feet, and were moving in a southwesterly direction.

They continued moving south as he watched them on a straight and level path, continuing southwest at a 240-degree heading, until they disappeared into the distance after about a minute and a half.

He reported that the pre-dawn early morning sky was clear, with no clouds or thunderstorms in the area.

He also alerted two ground radar installation sites in the area about the sighting. But he was told there were no radar images of the alleged objects.

The report doesn't list the name of the officer who prepared the report. That officer wrote that the only known air traffic at the time was heading east, not southwest.

Faltemeier told the reporting officer that two civilians had seen an unidentified object of the same description on the previous evening.

The operations officer had no comment on what he thought Faltemeier and the two civilians had seen.

It didn't appear that anyone from **Project Blue Book** tried to contact the two civilians.

An actual saucer?

But that's not all Faltemeier saw.

There's a second report in the **Project Blue Book** archives, that's also listed among the "unknowns."

The summary page of that report says that Faltemeier also saw a silver or white object the very next night — at 12:23 a.m. on Sept. 5, 1954.

He described it as having a slightly swept-back leading edge.

As it flew, it left an exhaust.

He saw it fly straight and level, then veer to the southwest and then to the south.

He was able to keep it in sight for 25-30 seconds until it headed south and faded from his view.

It was also listed as an unknown. The "electrical" report associated with Faltemeier's second UFO report goes into a little more detail.

From it we find out that he couldn't determine its exact shape, but when he held his hand up at arm's length, it was as long as one of his fingers. He first spotted it while he was checking the weather. Skies were clear that night and visibility was unrestricted.

He said the UFO had a "faint" light on it. And there was no sound as it passed overhead.

The report said there were also two B-47s in the sky at the time, but one was going east and the other was northeast — Faltemeier's UFO was going in the opposite direction, to the southwest. The operations officer reported that Faltemeier had also seen the other UFO (the string of lights) the previous night.

No follow-up

What I've noticed about some of these **Project Blue Book** cases is the lack of details and the lack of any more investigation.

For example, besides the form that the reporting officer filled out, there are no direct statements from Faltemeier and no apparent additional interviews with him about seeing what could have been an armada of 30 missiles, enemy craft or even invading flying saucers on one night and an even larger UFO the next night.

There also seemed to have been no attempt to contact the other two civilians who had seen the Butler lights on the previous night.

A reasonable person would have expected an investigator to check any news media in the vicinity, or with any law enforcement officers or dispatchers, to get more details.

However, the once-classified documents don't tell us if anyone else had reported a similar flying over Butler during the early morning darkness.

What's raises questions to researchers is seeing that both reports were simply marked as "unknowns" and "unidentified" then filed away.

Why? We know that the Air Force was taking such sightings seriously. We know that incompetence up and down the line of command was not the problem. Too many careers would have been at stake if they had all refused to look into matters involving the security of the airspace above the center of the country.

That leads me to believe that the Air Force knew what it was — perhaps a test of several high-flying secret aircraft?

Or it could have been that another agency, such as the CIA or the NSA, had taken over the case? Or did they know it was extraterrestrial and they preferred not to cause any public panic?

Without hard facts, all you have is rampant speculation and a never-ending suspicion that the government is hiding what it knows.

Despite the two UFOs being reported as "unidentified" at the time, it seems that after more than six decades the Air Force or the CIA would be able to clear up these sighting by admitting they were high-flying test flight of our own test aircraft, such as the U-2.

Unfortunately, that's not the case. And the Butler Lights on Sept. 4 and the Sept. 5 UFO remain two of the many 1954 real-life unsolved **Project Blue Book** X-files.

In the next chapter, we'll look at another puzzling UFO that was sighted less than three weeks later in the south-central historic Missouri town of Marshfield.

5. A baffling boomerang

MARSHFIELD, Missouri, (11 a.m. Sept. 22, 1954) — The two young men had just finished making a fuel delivery in south-central Missouri.

They were heading in a tank truck about three miles outside of the historic small town of Marshfield, Missouri, when they saw a lot of unusual objects high in the sky — including one that was fairly close.

The nearest object didn't look like a plane, a bird, or an aircraft.

If anything, it had sort of an asymmetrical "boomerang" shape. Part of one of the boomerang arms was slowly rotating.

As they watched, the puzzling object seem to tumble behind some trees and disappeared from their view. Later, some disturbances were found in the ground where it appeared to go down.

But as of this writing 64 years later, the Marshfield "boomerang" UFO these two men saw still remains unexplained, one of the 701 mysterious "unknowns" still unaccounted for in the Air Force's **Project Blue Book** once-classified files.

Famed astronomer's birthplace

There is nothing about Marshfield in particular that would stir up claims of strange UFO sightings or landings.

It's not really close to a known military base where secret aviation technology testing could have been taking place in late September 1954.

However, Marshfield does have one major claim to fame that puts it on the map for anybody who is serious about the study of astronomy.

The little town is the birthplace of perhaps the most famous cosmologist of the 20th century, Edwin Hubble.

Hubble had many achievements and honors during his lifetime. Those included being credited with discovering there are galaxies other than the Milky Way and that the universe is expanding — key concepts that have opened the way to space exploration and our understanding of the universe.

Outside astronomy circles, Hubble's name became well known to the general public in 1990 when NASA launched his namesake, the Hubble Space Telescope, into low-Earth orbit.

In memory of that event, a one-fourth-scale model of the HST sits on Marshfield's courthouse lawn.

Free of the visual disruptions of the Earth's atmosphere and weather systems, the HST's photographs of space objects have greatly expanded our study of distant galaxies.

And for UFO researchers, the HST's unblinking eye has also captured photos of unknown objects that have been fodder for speculation about extraterrestrial life or even conspiracies about our own secret military space operations.

I have not been able to find out whether the late astrophysicist himself ever saw or reported UFOs during the short time he lived in Marshfield.

Hubble's family away moved from Marshfield in 1900 when he was a boy. However, his biographers do say that he had a strong interest in astronomy since his boyhood.

Hubble spent most of his adult life in Pasadena, California, on the staff of the Mount Wilson Observatory.

He died at the age of 63 in September 1953 — nearly a year before the "boomerang" UFO sighting took place over Marshfield.

Men in black?

Unlike some of the other **Project Blue Book** unknowns, which include only basic details, the Marshfield sighting seems rich in documentation — with 39 pages found in the files. It includes two sketches. It has standard UFO reporting forms filled out by the two witnesses. And there are narratives written by investigators.

That seemed strange, because by that time, the **Project Blue Book** office was mostly a report-taking unit, with only a few personnel.

However, a once-confidential USAF report from January 1954 indicates the Air Force was turning any major UFO field investigations over to a new group, a secretive military unit that now seems to be the basis for the UFO folklore surrounding the mysterious "men in black" — the 4602d Air Intelligence Service Squadron.

Based out of Ent Air Force Base in Colorado Springs, Colorado, the 4602d consisted of small teams of personnel with experience at recovering captured or crashed military aircraft or missiles from foreign countries.

The once-secret report from 1954 indicated that the 4602d, activated in March 1952, was responsible for any UFO reports within the continental 48 states. The squadron would report its investigations to the Air Technical Investigations Command at Wright-Patterson Air Force Base in Dayton, Ohio.

And the investigators were charged with secrecy — they could tell no one who they were or call attention to themselves — *"absolutely no publicity is to be given to the Squadron mission or to individuals within the Squadron ... in other words, stay away from publicity ..."*

Some UFO researchers have speculated the 4602d investigators are likely the basis of the "men in black" characters portrayed by Will Smith and Tommy Lee Jones in the three Hollywood "Men in Black" films.

You can imagine characters in dark business suits showing up at the Marshfield sighting, taking charge, interviewing witnesses and then disappearing.

Documents show the Marshfield investigation took more than two months. The final 39-page Marshfield report was filed on Dec. 2, 1954. It was filed by USAF Capt. Milton Bellovin, who at the time was with the 4602d.

Tiny silver dots

The names of the two witnesses had been blotted out on some of the forms now available to the public online.

Fortunately, researchers affiliated with the non-government UFO research organization NICAP (National Investigative Committee for Aerial Phenomenon) had access to the documents several years before the names were redacted. NICAP reports the names of the two witnesses as Ernest J. Ash and Jack N. Williams, who both lived in Marshfield.

According to the **Project Blue Book** reports, Williams, the manager for the Webster Gas Company, and Ash, another employee, had finished up a delivery job in Bracken, Mo., and were in a tank truck heading back west toward Marshfield.

Ash was looking out the window at the sky. He spotted groupings of strange objects first and then pointed them out to Williams, who was driving.

Up in the sky, they saw three groups of tiny silver dots that appeared to be at an extreme height.

The documents include a three-page first-person account of the event, which was signed by both Williams and Ash.

That three-page document, which had a few mistakes and spelling errors, was typed on the gas company's stationery.

Williams wrote that their unusual encounter began about 11 a.m. His description of the area indicates they were traveling west on what is now Missouri State Highway DD, approaching the road leading into the Arrowhead Scout Camp.

"Approximately three miles east of Marshfield, Missouri, on what is known as the Scout Camp Road, we observed far to the west 3 clouds or formations of silver objects," Williams wrote.

"They were far enough away or so small that they appeared as no more than a silver dot to our eyes, their [there] *were, as a rough guess, many thousands of these objects."*

Williams wrote that he stopped the truck to watch the objects.

A closer, rotating object

After about two minutes, Ash noticed another object at what they guessed to be 600 feet high and about 200 yards to the southwest.

"This object was somewhat like a boomerang in shape with the exception that one side or wing was very short and the other side or wing much longer," he wrote.

He guessed the object's entire width was about six to seven feet.

"This object was very thin in the wing section and the body as well," he wrote. It was also silent. And it appeared to be covered or made of some sort of plastic or very thin material.

"It revolved very slowly, the entire object revolved, not just the one wing," he wrote. *"As it revolved and the wing came around near the sun it seemed to shine through or nearly through because of the change in color, it would seem to be much lighter in color when the sun was behind it."*

He wrote the color was a dark tan, with two black stripes near the end of the wing or rotor.

"After we watched the object for a few minutes it started a climb without changing its flight characteristics or without gaining any RPM of its wing," Williams wrote. *"After rising to what we thought to be about 1,500 feet it then started to come down much slower than it had climbed."* The climb had taken only about 20 seconds.

After coming down to what Williams and Ash thought was about 500 feet, the object changes its revolving *action "in that it started tumbling but not any faster than it had revolved."*

Then it did something even more strange.

"After falling a short distance in this position it emitted a puff of white smoke or vapor," Williams wrote. He explained it was *"not in a trailing form but just one bigg* [big] *puff of smoke or vapor."*

At the time the smoke appeared, it still made no noise. It had been silent the entire time they watched.

"After emitting this smoke or vapor it stopped all motion and fell straight into a small patch of timber," Williams wrote.

They did not actually see the object hit the ground because of the rough terrain, but they did see it go behind the timberline.

"We then left out [our] *truck and went into the woods to see if we could find any other trace of this object,"* Williams wrote. After some minutes (he didn't say how many) they found *"two places in the earth completely pulverized."*

There were no signs of animal tracks near the pulverized area.

"This might or might not have had anything to do with it but it did seem strange in such soft dirt that if an animal or human had made it that it did not leave any track," Williams wrote.

Williams backtracked to give more information about the object before it disappeared.

"When we first noticed this object, it seemed to hover at about the 600 feet level." The wing or rotor was slightly curved upward at the tip and near the two dark stripes. When the rotation stopped and the object started to fall, the wing or rotor was pointed up, *"indicating the base of this wing, which would be the body, was the heaviest part,"* Williams wrote.

The strange object moved slowly.

"At no time was there much speed involved in any fashion," he wrote. *"While falling, it did not flutter or turn at all, but fell straight down behind the timber line. Before falling past the timber line we watched this object for about 15 minutes."*

After they searched the area very thoroughly, they returned to Marshfield and Williams called the Fordland Air Force Station, which was set up in 1951 as a radar station.

Williams talked with the chief warrant officer, A.R. Justman, about the object.

Justman, who was also the public information officer, then sent four men to Marshfield where they picked up Williams and Ash.

They returned to the area and made a more thorough search of a much wider area, but without finding any more trace of the object.

Later, about 6 pm., Justman and Williams both went out a third time to try to find the object.

However, they still failed to find anything other than the two places in the earth that appeared to be pulverized.

What became of the initial silver objects they saw?

"After leaving the truck in the beginning to start the first search, Mr. Ash and myself did not see the silver objects again that first attracted our attention," Williams wrote. *"The two of us had time to study the object and it is just as I have described it."*

Investigation continues

In many of the Air Force investigations, that would have been the end of it. **Project Blue Book** would gather information, thank the source and try to explain it away, or mark it as unidentified, then move on.

But the sincerity of the two men — and the utter strangeness of what they saw — seemed to have spurred the Air Force into going further.

On Oct. 4, Justman, the chief warrant officer, sent his findings off to Capt. Charles A. Hart at ATIC's offices at Wright-Patterson AFB in Dayton, Ohio.

Justman's memo indicates he thought it might have been a helicopter. Justman writes that he had contacted Capt. Basye at Fort Leonard Wood earlier on Oct. 4, who told Justman there had been no helicopter activity at the time of the sighting.

"Captain Basye states that a Helicopter could be dispatched to UFOB area for reconnaissance, if desired," Justman wrote.

Another document in the report indicates that someone at ATIC must have stewed over the information and the sketches that Williams and Ash made of their UFO.

It shows they turned it over to the 4602d. And two months after the sighting, the 4602d sent investigators (possibly dressed in black suits and ties) down to Marshfield to see what else they could find.

The report, filed by USAF Capt. Milton Bellovin, who was with Detachment 2 of the OIC, said the technical investigator, Master Sgt. Frazie Noe, obtained information from sources on Nov. 22, 1954, at Marshfield — and that Noe considered them to be "reliable."

In his report about Noe's investigation, Bellovin writes that Williams and Ash were certain they had observed the object for 15 minutes.

"The condition of sky was bright with sun at SOURCES right when object was observed."

Bellovin writes the object was tan, contrasting to the blue background of the sky.

"Object appeared to stand still then go up and come down with a pulsation, emitting puffs of white smoke," he wrote. *"It did not change shape, brightness, nor did it break up or explode. Object did not move in front of anything at any time."*

Bellovin wrote that the object was silent, had two black stripes near the end of the protrusion and the edges of the object were sharply outlined as it rotated counter-clockwise.

The sources told Noe they were fairly certain that the object appeared to be the size of a grapefruit when held at arm's length, or about five feet in overall length (although their later sketches show it was six to eight feet long).

The witnesses weren't able to tell Noe what kind of material it could have been constructed of, but that one of the men said he could make a model of it with modeling clay.

Bellovin wrote that the object was first seen while they were driving in the open countryside. Williams told Noe he was driving west at 20 mph when Ash first noticed the object, about 225 degrees from true north and 45 degrees above the horizon.

They stopped the truck, got out and kept watching, Bellovin wrote. The UFO was 190 degrees from true north and 10 degrees above the horizon when it disappeared.

Weather conditions were hot and dry, with a clear sky and a slight breeze. Both witnesses told Noe they had never seen an object like that before. They couldn't give him an estimate of the object's speed. Williams estimated they were between 450 and 900 feet away from it.

Bellovin's report says that Williams, besides being the manager for the Webster Gas Co., was 28 years old, was a high school graduate and had attended an armored school while in the Army.

Williams *"seemed to be very intelligent, sober and sincere. He was very definite in his statements of what he had seen,"* Noe wrote. *"He holds a private pilot's license and is quite familiar with aircraft. Mr. Williams is also a model airplane enthusiast. Investigator questioned Mr. Williams as to the possibility of object having been a model airplane and received a negative reply."*

Bellovin also wrote that Ernest Ash was a tank truck driver for the same gas company, was 21 years old and was a grade school graduate. Ash corroborated statements made by Williams.

Unexplained fire

Bellovin's report indicates he checked to see if anything unusual was happening in Marshfield at that time. He found that approximately two hours after the UFO sighting, a fire was reported in the city dump.

"This dump lay in the direct line of travel of the object when last seen," Bellovin reported. *"Origin of fire was never determined nor any connection established between it and the object."*

Noe, the investigator, asked Williams and Ash if the UFO they saw was large enough for crewmembers of average size to fit inside. They told him no.

"Investigator was unable to determine what the object was or what its origin could have been from the limited information received," Bellovin wrote.

Bellovin's report and a copy of the AF Form 112 report, a technical information questionnaire the witnesses filled out, was then forwarded to ATIC for further analysis and evaluation.

Two sketches

The report included two fairly detailed sketches. The sketches showed the object's unusual shape, its length and width, how it rotated counter-clockwise and what part of it emitted white smoke before it fell.

The first sketch seemed to have been done in pencil, possibly by Ash.

The second sketch seemed more finished, as if it were inked and neatly hand lettered in a mechanical drawing style.

It's possible Williams drew the second sketch because the lettering matches his handwriting on the AF Form 112 he filled out.

Both drawings indicate the object was about 2.5 feet wide and about four to five inches thick.

Williams completed his questionnaire and sent it to Air Force CWO R.C. Schum, the assistant adjudant at ATIC, according to a memo Williams typed on his company's stationery, dated Nov. 22, 1954.

Williams offered to provide any assistance in the future if they needed it.

Hynek puzzled by sighting

The **Project Blue Book** files don't contain any other information about the object or if the "men in black" of the 4602d did any more investigation.

But the sighting was clearly a puzzle to J. Allen Hynek, the astrophysicist and professor at Ohio State University who at the time was the Air Force's go-to outside scientific adviser for UFO sightings. When he began working for the Air Force Hynek was mainly used as a UFO debunker. But as more strange reports came his way to analyze, he began to develop an open mind on the subject.

Hynek's 1977 book, *The Hynek UFO Report*, on page 178, refers to what Williams and Ash saw as *"The Case of the Leisurely Boomerang."*

Hynek starts off by saying he was always impressed that mature adults with respectable positions would report the most incredible tales and that they had no motive for perpetrating a hoax. And he asks how could you write off something as a hallucination that was seen by two or more people?

He goes on to relate the statements of Williams and the investigators. Then he gives his own analysis:

"A rotating, boomerang-like propeller, maneuvering by itself in the daytime air does not fit the general UFO pattern," Hynek wrote. *"One gets the feeling that the UFO phenomenon, whatever it may be, is indeed 'playing games with us' and leading us a merry chase."*

Some 40 years after he wrote that, the "merry chase" continues.

PART 3:

FEAR & FANTASY

By the late 1950s, UFOs were on the public's mind as both a threat and as a subject of fantasy. The public was getting news reports about UFOs mixed in with the Cold War reports between the Soviet Union and the U.S., plus a wealth of science fiction stories in magazines, paperbacks and movies about unknown creatures and the harm they might do.

For that reason, some witnesses found it a sense of duty to file a report, for fear of an invasion. Meanwhile, others didn't want to come forward out of fear of what they had experienced or possibly fear of looking ridiculous.

Chapters 6 and 7 in this book cover two **Project Blue Book** unknowns from that time that seem to indicate both of those sentiments.

6. **A dozen discs**

ST. LOUIS, Missouri (6:10 a.m. Nov. 17, 1955) — Imagine the strange sight in front of J. A. Mapes as he walked outside on that cool crisp fall morning.

There in the pre-dawn sky was something unusual. It was something peculiar. It was something that just didn't make any sense.

In fact, it might even pose a threat.

What the St. Louis man and his wife saw in the light of the morning sky just before sunrise probably shook them up — a dozen discs flying in a four-deep formation over their home for nearly a minute.

What should they do? What would any of us do?

I can imagine the pointing, the questions they had and the conversation they had after the sighting.

"Are they flying saucers?"

"But aren't those just a joke — just something everybody's been laughing about for a few years?"

"But we know what we're seeing. These are real."

"Then what else could they be?"

"Maybe they're ours. Maybe the Air Force is testing secret aircraft? I've never seen a plane move like that."

"What if they're Russian? What if they came in over Canada? Maybe we're in danger. Shouldn't we tell somebody?"

Unfortunately, we don't know what conversation the couple had that morning over their morning coffee. In fact, we don't have hardly any information about the St. Louis couple or their backgrounds. But what we do know is the sight must have been very unsettling to them. It was enough for them to put themselves out there — and risk the ridicule of authorities.

Like thousands of other Americans who had seen such sights across the country, Mapes decided he owed it to himself and to the country to go ahead and take the unusual step of reporting what he saw to the Air Force. While the couple themselves may have stayed in the background, their story has not — it is one of the 701 sightings that the Air Force's **Project Blue Book** has marked as unidentified.

Political climate

Thanks to the diligence of private organizations like NICAP, the once-hidden-away **Project Blue Book** files are available online to analyze.

Unfortunately, the files of many of the cases, including this one, are somewhat meager. Part of the reason is that after the first few years the amount of manpower devoted to **Project Blue Book** was reduced significantly.

By 1955, many officials in the Air Force wanted to shut down the formal investigation, saying that the existence of a **Project Blue Book** gave flying saucers a status that they didn't deserve.

And there had been subtle efforts to belittle those who reported such tales of flying saucers or alien beings as simple-minded people who were letting their imaginations — and what they were seeing the popular culture — get the better of them.

Ruppelt's book

If there was an official line to downplay the sightings, it began seeing a lot of pushback.

In the world of UFO investigations at the time, 1956 was a breakthrough year in that a former insider gave us the background on the Air Force's study of UFOs.

About two months after the Mapes couple's sighting, Doubleday published a book by Capt. Edward J. Ruppelt, former head of **Project Blue Book**.

The eye-opening book is titled ***The Report on Unidentified Flying Objects.***

Ruppelt's book lays out his findings from two years of analyzing UFO reports and talking to UFO witnesses, who included *"industrialists, pilots, engineers, generals, and just the plain man-on-the-street."*

Ruppelt pointed out that while the Air Force's official position was that there was no proof an interplanetary spaceship existed, the conclusion was *"far from unanimous among the military and their scientific advisers."*

A famous quote from his book is about what constitutes the proof — short of aliens or crashed ships — that UFOs exist:

"Does a UFO have to land at the River Entrance to the Pentagon, near the Joint Chiefs of Staff offices? Or is it proof when a ground radar station detects a UFO, sends a jet to intercept it, the jet pilot sees it, and locks on with his radar, only to have the UFO streak away at a phenomenal speed? Is it proof when a jet pilot fires at a UFO and sticks to his story even under the threat of court-martial? Does this constitute proof?"

Ruppelt's book indicated that not only was the jury still out on the subject, but the military had much more information than it was letting the public know.

UFOs at the box office

Sometimes it's also interesting to look at the context of what the witnesses might have experienced before seeing something unusual.

If Mapes and his wife were regular moviegoers, they had many opportunities to see how UFOs were interpreted in their day by Hollywood.

By November 1955, theaters around the country had been showing a movie that over the ensuing decades has become a sci-fi classic — *"This Island Earth."*

The film includes flying saucers, a green menacing tractor beam, deadly rays that could blow up cars, humanoids with white hair and high foreheads, and the threat of what's out in the universe.

Could Mapes and his wife have seen *"This Island Earth"* and made references to it before deciding to call the authorities?

Ike's 'Open Skies 'proposal

The couple might also have been reading their morning paper about threats of what the Russians were planning on the other side of the globe.

Newspapers across the country on that day were running banner front-page headlines about the "failure" of the recent "Big Four" (the U.S., the Soviet Union, Great Britain, and France) conference in Geneva, Switzerland — and predictions of an ensuing stepped-up "Cold War" between the East and West.

Actually, the Geneva Summit of 1955 had been set up as a way to cool tensions and mistrust among the four powers emerging from World War II, and would later prove to be successful along those lines.

However, at that particular time, the mistrust between the Soviet Union and the U.S. was moving toward its peak. And the Soviets had rejected U.S. President Dwight D. Eisenhower's proposal for "Open Skies."

Eisenhower's goal was to slow down the arms race and the buildup of nuclear arsenals in the U.S. and the Soviet Union.

U.S. military analysts believed that the Soviet Union would within 10 years have the ability to wipe out the U.S. in a surprise nuclear strike.

And there were those in the U.S.'s own military who thought our best option was to strike first.

Fortunately, Ike chose the diplomatic solution.

Ike's Open Skies proposal called for revealing what your side had and allowing the other side to verify it. Each country would be allowed unarmed observation flights to keep track of what military operations were going on inside the other country in order to make sure they weren't preparing for an attack.

However, Soviet Premier Nikita Khrushchev rejected the proposal when it was first introduced in the July 1955 conference. (It wasn't until 1992 that an Open Skies treaty was finally reached between the parties.)

The second part of the Geneva conference took place in the fall of 1955, but efforts to reunify German at the time failed to make any progress.

Project Dragon Lady

Meanwhile, as the U.S. sought diplomatic ways to check up on the Soviets, they were secretly working on a way to do so through technology.

For several months before Mapes' UFO sighting, the CIA had been working with the Air Force and Lockheed engineers at Area 51 in Nevada to develop a high-flying spy plane.

Associated with colorful codenames such as "Project DRAGON LADY", "Project AQUATONE" and "Project OILSTONE," the U-2 spy plane was under testing in Area 51 by the fall of 1955.

An internal history monograph of the U-2, *THE CENTRAL INTELLIGENCE AGENCY AND OVERHEAD RECONNAISSANCE: THE U-2 AND OXCART PROGRAMS, 1954-1974*, was written in the 1980s by CIA historians Gregory W. Pedlow and Donald E. Welzenbach.

Published as a classified document in 1992, Pedlow and Welzenbach's monograph was finally declassified in 2013. *(As of this writing, a pdf document with blacked-out redacted sections referring to Area 51 was available on the CIA public website at* **https://www.cia.gov/library/center-for-the-study-of-intelligence/csi-publications/books-and-monographs/the-cia-and-the-u-2-program-1954-1974/u2.pdf.***)*

Pedlow and Welzenbach's history says the first U-2 plane was delivered in July 1955 to Area 51, which was picked as a remote site where the reconnaissance plane could be fine-tuned and tested.

The official "first flight" was made Aug. 8, 1955. And a month later, they reached 65,600 feet.

The Pedlow and Welzenbach history says that the U-2 secret test flights at above 60,000 feet began generating reports of UFOs in the skies after that period — the public didn't know we had planes that could fly that high.

Pedlow and Welzenbach estimated that around half of the UFO reports coming into **Project Blue Book** during the late 1950s and the majority of the 1960s could be attributed to tests of the U-2 and the later Project OXCART flights.

I had hoped to find if any of the U-2 cross-country tests could have been on the same date as Mapes's Nov. 17, 1955, UFO sighting over St. Louis.

However, the Pedlow and Welzenbach report indicated that the testing during that time involved the pressurized suits, the high-end camera operation and learning to fly the spy plane at 60,000 feet-plus altitudes, most of which seemed to have taken place in and around the remote airspace of Area 51. There was nothing related to the U-2 at that time around St. Louis, according to their history.

Their U-2 history indicates the Strategic Air Command didn't order a fleet of the high-flying spy planes until early 1956. The over-flight tests across the U.S. didn't begin until April 1956.

So it's doubtful the Mapes couple's sighting of the 12 discs were U-2 spy planes — not that many U-2s had yet been delivered to Groom Lake.

Crash on the same date

However, there was a strange and somewhat chilling coincidence contained in Pedlow and Welzenbach's history.

To get the U-2 engineers and personnel out to the remote Area 51 testing facility, a Military Air Transport Service (MATS) flight had begun making regular shuttle trips out of Burbank, California, in October.

On Nov. 17, 1955 — the same days Mapes reported the fleet of flying saucers over St. Louis — a MATS flight taking personnel from Burbank to the U-2 testing grounds at Area 51 crashed at Mount Charleston, just west of Las Vegas.

It was a major tragedy. All 14 people aboard were killed, including the project security officer, the CIA's William H. Marr, four members of his staff and others.

The CIA historians called it *"the greatest single loss of life in the entire U-2 program."*

The crash has always been attributed to an early winter storm in the area — the pilot, who did not have access to modern-day navigational instruments, is thought to have become disoriented as he piloted the aircraft through a winter storm through Kyle Canyon.

However, one UFO researcher's study of military crashes during the 1950s makes me wonder if there might have been another cause for that tragic crash in Kyle Canyon.

Author and UFO researcher Timothy Good has written that many of the military aircraft crashes that occurred during the 1950s could have been interactions between Air Force pilots and UFOs.

In his book, *Need to Know, UFOs, Military and Intelligence* (p. 178), Good writes there were more than 18,600 military crashes during the mid 1950s, with about 9.5 percent (1,773) of them attributed to "unknown" factors.

Could the Kyle Canyon crash on the same day as the Mapes sighting have been one of these?

Good has never suggested it himself, from what I've seen of his writings. And all the news reports of the Kyle Canyon crash indicates weather caused the tragedy.

Could it have been more than a tragic accident?

Could that secret flight of top U-2 personnel have been shot down by a squadron of 12 flying discs seen that same day by Mapes over Missouri?

Were they merely birds?

Project Blue Book has only four pages on Mapes' sighting. It's not clear if anyone even thought it should be investigated further.

The Project 10073 Record Card (ATIC form 329) gives the time as 1210Z (which is military Zulu time for 6:10 a.m.) on Thursday, Nov. 17, 1955.

It says 12 UFOs were observed from the ground by a civilian (Mapes) for 45 seconds and that no photos were taken.

The UFOs were described as *"Round and flat, dark on bottom side, silver colored on top side, 3 abreast, four deep. No sound. Initial observation at 75 deg elev in NE, disappearing over horizon in NE."*

In the *"Conclusions"* area, which gave the analyst a chance to mark whether it was a balloon, an aircraft or an astronomical occurrence, the analyst placed an *"X"* in the check box for *"Unknown."* And under *"other"* they also typed in *"UNIDEN-TIFIED."*

The only clue we have as to why they didn't seem to investigate further was in the comments area, where someone typed the words *"UNIDENTIFIED (Birds??)"*

The only other documents associated with the case are three all-caps pages from the "electrical" report, a telecommunications message that was designed to immediately notify in writing the pertinent officials in U.S. air defense command around the country and at ATIC headquarters at Wright-Patterson Air Force Base in Dayton, Ohio.

The electrical report contains responses to the questions in AFR-200, the standardized Air Force regulation checklist prepared for officers investigating *"UFOBs."*

Besides being silver on the top and dark on the bottom, the checklist responses say each of the 12 round flat objects were about the size a baseball would appear to be when held up at arm's length.

The responses say there were no discernable features or details to the UFOs other than they were in a formation three abreast and four deep. The UFOs also left behind no tail, trail or exhaust trail behind them.

For as large as they were — and as many — they made no sound. *"No vibration or signs of type of power units observed,"* the electrical report said.

What drew Mapes' attention to them in the early morning sky? *"Brightness of one side caught observer's eye,"* was the answer.

As they flew off to the northeast, *"objects appeared to fly in formation but tipped from horizontal to vertical and from left to right."*

Then, after about 45 seconds, they disappeared over the horizon.

Mapes, whose name was blotted out on the form, was 64 years old and was listed as semi-retired. His wife was listed as a 60-year-old housewife.

In terms of the weather, the report indicates the sky was clear and the early morning sun was shining, with only a few scattered clouds.

Secret new aircraft?

One reason that there might have been no follow-up is that the Air Force investigator thought it might have been some new, secret type of aircraft being developed.

The electrical report says there were no scheduled flights of aircraft that were in the vicinity that day.

But in the next line, the unnamed *"wing intelligence officer"* making the report was asked to make his own assessment of the sighting.

He wrote *"Possible cause of sighting new type of aircraft in formation."*

We know now it wasn't a fleet of U-2s.

As noted earlier in this chapter, the first secret tests weren't until the following April, according to the CIA's now declassified history of the program.

And even if it had been a group of U-2 spy plane prototypes, they wouldn't have been that big — at 60,000 feet, they would be more like a speck in the sky rather than the size of baseballs.

So that takes us right back to where we started.

We still don't know whose silver flying discs were silently zipping across St. Louis, staying in formation, on that early November morning in 1955.

And it's still marked with an X on the books as an *"unknown."*

The next chapter deals with a reluctant witness who had an encounter over a small arms manufacturing facility near Kansas City.

7. Disabling a car

LAKE CITY, Missouri (Nov. 9, 1957) — Imagine driving home from your job on a cold November night, then confronting something extraordinary — a large luminous object hovering above the roadway.

What is it, you wonder? A plane?

Or could it be a balloon? Could your eyes be playing tricks on you? No, it's real. It's up there. As you drive closer to it, you become uneasy.

Then suddenly, your car abruptly shuts down. You try, but the engine won't turn over. There's no spark. What's going on?

You look up. The strange oval object — you don't even want to think it might be one of those crazy flying saucers — is still there. Did that thing overhead kill your engine? Who — or what — could do that?

Suddenly you feel uneasy. Trapped.

Are you now at the mercy at whatever's up there, be it a friend, a foe, or even a predator? A chill comes over you. All you can do is watch it and wonder what comes next.

Many other sightings

Nearly 60 years ago as of this writing, that strange UFO encounter happened to a Blue Springs, Missouri, man whose story is still unsolved.

Unfortunately, we don't have the man's full identity, only his last name, "Boardman," from a document in the **Project Blue Book** files.

The man might have felt very alone and vulnerable peering up into the night sky from inside his car. But we know now he wasn't alone in seeing something peculiar on that date. **Project Blue Book** lists 28 UFO reports from that day, sightings that took place across the country.

Those sightings included four others from Missouri, all of which were explained away by **Project Blue Book** analysts, who were from both inside and outside the military.

One of those four other UFOs reported on that date, in Seneca, Missouri, was dismissed as an aircraft. Another UFO, over in Arcadia, Missouri, was explained away as the planet Venus. Two others from that date were thought to have been a meteor falling (St. Louis and Danby).

A fifth one on that date was in Belton, Missouri. But the documents from that case are missing from the files. The Belton case, like the one from Lake City, is marked *"insufficient data."*

Why *"insufficient data?"*

For reference, the designation "Insufficient data" was assigned by **Project Blue Book** to a UFO case that didn't have enough information for an Air Force investigator or an outside scientist/analyst to either explain away the sighting (as a balloon, an aircraft, birds, or something natural astronomical occurrence, like a planet or a meteor)— or designate it as an *"unknown"* or *"unidentified."*

Besides the Lake City case, it's interesting that there were six other *"insufficient data"* sightings on Nov. 9, 1957, across the country among the 28 UFOs reported to **Project Blue Book**.

A preponderance of evidence?

When you look through the case files, it appears the evidence was stacking up (28 sightings) that something unusual was happening in the skies on that particular date across the country.

So a re-examination of the sightings might be in order.

Could the analysts have been wrong not to place more of the sightings into the *"unknown"* category rather than the politically innocuous *"insufficient data"* category?

Or there could have been another reason: Did the military already know what was going on?

The Lake City case, in all probability, would have ended up as an official *"unknown"* or *"unidentified"* real-life X file cases except for one thing: the witness was reluctant to talk to **Project Blue Book** investigators about it.

Third-hand information

As stated earlier, we know very little about the witness. But we can read into some of the documentation that he didn't want to talk about it to anybody official.

So that raises some red flags and raises some skepticism: Did it actually happen? Could this merely be a story the man told his wife to cover for what he was really doing?

Or did it really happen and he just didn't want to appear foolish? Could it have it shaken him up so much he couldn't talk about it?

According to the **Project Blue Book** 10073 Record Card on the Lake City case, we know that it was reported to have happened at 1 a.m. on Nov. 9, 1957. And we know that there were no photos taken to corroborate what he saw.

Making and testing bullets

A reasonable question is why would a large oval UFO be flying over Lake City? Was it looking for something?

For geographical reference, Lake City is near Independence, Missouri, just east of the Kansas City metropolitan area.

Since 1941, it has been the site of an Army small arms munitions plant that was being operated at the time of the UFO sighting in 1957 by Remington Arms as the contractor.

Then known as the Lake City Arsenal, Lake City was the first of a dozen small-arms plants operated by the Army around the country.

As of this writing, the current Lake City Army Ammunition Plant is housed on 3,935 acres, with 408 buildings, and has a staff of nearly 30 people, mostly Army staff civilians.

As of this writing, it's the military's largest producer of small-arms ammunition and serves as the NATO National and Regional Test Center.

The Army says the plant can make small arms cartridges, components such as percussion and electric primers, pyrotechnics and small-caliber ammunition. It also is capable of disposing of plant-produced small-caliber ammunition and explosives and performs reliability testing of small-caliber ammunition.

Bringing in the FBI

Although the Air Force was the official government agency charged with investigating UFOs at the time, we know that other agencies were also involved.

In this case, the documents associated with the case contain a letter dated Nov. 14, 1957, from FBI Special Agent in Charge Percy Wyly II.

Wyly, who was based in Kansas City, Missouri, notified the district commander of the Office of Special Investigations at the U.S. Air Force's Offutt Air Base in Omaha, Nebraska, about the incident.

Wyly's two-page letter says that on Nov. 13, Lester Scott, the chief supervisor of protection, Lake City Arsenal, Lake City, Missouri, informed Wyly that the Blue Springs man (whose name was redacted on the copy of the letter) *"saw an unidentified flying object near the Pink Hill Grocery store south of Lake City Arsenal about 1 a.m. November 9, 1957."*

Afraid to speak up

The person who could be thought of as the hero — or whistleblower — of this tale was the witness's wife, who goes unnamed in the FBI special agent's letter.

The heavily redacted letter says the witness' wife *"related the story of her husband's observation to Mr. [redacted] an employee at Lake City Arsenal, and stated that her husband did not intend to report his observations **because no one would believe him.**"* (My emphasis.)

So we have one, the man who didn't want to subject himself to ridicule; two, his wife who heard this incredible story and thought someone should know; three, an apparent family friend who was also an employee at the plant, who also thought someone should know; and four, Lester Scott, who must have been their boss and thought the FBI ought to get to the bottom of this strange incident.

Back to the FBI agent's letter: In the next paragraph Wyly gives a short synopsis of the story.

"Allegedly, [the witness] *was driving his automobile from his place of employment, somewhere in Kansas City area, to his home when he observed the unidentified object hovering about fifty feet off the ground. The object was oval in shape. As* [the witness] *approached the object, the engine of his automobile died and would not function again until the object moved on."*

And, like the witness, Wyly apparently didn't want to go any further with the story.

"No additional inquiry or investigation is being conducted concerning the matter by this office," Wyly wrote.

I can't tell by Wyly's letter how he got his information.

Because his retelling sounds so basic, it seems doubtful he actually personally interviewed the witness. It's also difficult to tell whether Wyly was open to the idea the man actually saw something, or if Wyly was merely fulfilling an obligation to pass on the information to J. Edgar Hoover, then the director of the FBI.

A similar case

What's interesting is that Wyly's letter made it into the **Project Blue Book** files. That indicates there may have been some coordination going on between the Air Force and the FBI.

The document in the **Blue Book** files also shows that someone, possibly the commander at Offutt Air Base or an analyst, penned some notes on Wyly's typed letter.

The words *"oval in shape"* about the UFO are circled.

And the words *"engine of his automobile died"* are underlined, with that line extending down to a notation in cursive that reads in part, *"Follows same pattern of persons who have been reading about the 'Blue Light Stops Cars' in the papers for the last two weeks. Suggestibility!"*

Newspaper stories

That notation was apparently a reference to the newspaper stories about a similar case in Levelland, Texas, that had occurred about a week earlier.

In that 1957 **Project Blue Book** case, which occurred during the night of Nov. 2 and early morning on Nov. 3, several people in Levelland, Texas, reported seeing a low-flying glowing object, about 100 feet long, in the sky.

Some thought it was an airplane about to crash. Some reported that their car headlights and radio shut down, or their engine sputtered for a short time as the object passed overhead.

The case got a lot of attention the next few days in the media as witnesses flooded the police, sheriff and fire departments with phone calls.

Curiously, a **Blue Book** investigator spent only about seven hours interviewing witnesses. He concluded there were storms in the area and wrote off the auto failures and the sightings as the result of "ball lightning."

However, that analysis has been criticized over subsequent years by follow-up UFO investigators who pointed out there were no storms that night.

Why would a **Project Blue Book** analyst have dismissed such a flurry of sightings as the result of ball lightning? Were they told not to look into it any further? Were they working with the CIA?

The CIA now admits it used UFO sightings as a cover explanation for high-flying U-2 spy plane sightings seen in the 1950s and 1960s. However, that would not account for the low-flying craft in the Lake City or Levelland sightings.

What the Lake City sighting shows us is that there might have been several other people who saw it.

Maybe they were like the reluctant witness — they didn't want to tell what they saw because they didn't think anyone would believe them.

A return trip?

The Lake City ammunition plant has also had other sightings not recorded in **Project Blue Book** — including an eerily similar event that happened 12 years later.

Margie Kay, assistant state director for Missouri MUFON's Kansas City office put out a press release in June 2014 that was published online by the Kansas City Star and KGRAradio.com.

Kay wrote that the Missouri MUFON organization had received a report that "a large UFO" was seen in 1969 hovering over the Lake City plant — at the same time electric power was knocked out at the plant.

"The witness, who was told to keep quiet about the event, recently decided to come forward in order to let the public know that an unidentified object hovered and moved about the plant for two hours in the middle of the night and was witnessed by at least 13 people," says the press release.

The prime witness was Raymond Griggs, who was 22 years old at the time of the 1969 sighting. Griggs was then living in Independence, Missouri, and was working as a civilian contractor in the plant's print shop.

"On a hot August night in 1969, the electricity for the entire plant and all buildings suddenly went out, so the crew of seven in his department went outside to cool down. That is when they noticed a UFO.

"A bright chrome spherical object hovered just over a building which was located four buildings away from the men's position. The object then slowly moved over another building across the road and hovered, then continued to zigzag back and forth across the road from building to building for approximately two hours. The seven men on the crew with Mr. Griggs talked amongst themselves while watching the UFO. At the same time, several jeeps with MPs were driving to and from the area very quickly ..."

The UFO *"... then left the area by shooting up into the sky at a 30-degree angle at an incredible speed."*

Griggs claimed it was gone in one-half of a second — its speed made all the witnesses believe that it couldn't be a military aircraft. He said that as soon as the UFO left, the electricity at the plant was restored.

According to the MUFON report, the next morning two unknown men who didn't identify themselves arrived at the office. One was dressed in a gray suit, while one was in black.

The witnesses were assembled and were told, *"Remember that you have all signed a security clearance and you did not see anything."* The two men who gave the orders then turned and left.

Griggs said the message was clear — and that he did not tell anyone about the experience for 45 years. He told MUFON he decided to come forward after seeing an episode of the History Channel's "Hangar 1: The UFO Files" TV series involving sightings investigated by MUFON around Kansas City.

That particular episode spurred others to speak out, the MUFON press release says: *"In the past several days six more witnesses have come forward about similar UFO sightings over and near Lake City Army Ammo Plant in 2001, 2013, and 2014."*

One further note: The more I research the UFO subject, the deeper and more interesting it gets. I was pleased to see I wasn't the only one who thought this case should have been classified as an "unknown" rather than as an "insufficient data" case.

Brad Sparks of NICAP has included this case among his catalog of "unknowns," which go far beyond the 701 cases labeled as unknowns by **Project Blue Book**.

Also, UFO researcher Jaques Valleé lists the 1957 Lake City case in the appendix of his book, ***Passport to Magonia, From Folklore to Flying Saucers.***

PART 4:

CRITICISM MOUNTS

The continuation of the secret high-flying spy planes and spy satellites travelling over the Soviet Union may have accounted for some UFO sightings during the mid to late 1950s. However, credible people were still seeing incredibly unexplainable things — and making reports to **Project Blue Book**.

But **Project Blue Book's** limited response was under fire by critics. By the 1960s, its staff was miniscule. And the top brass in the Air Force seemed to want to get out from under public scrutiny about their UFO studies.

The public might have thought the Air Force was thoroughly investigating reports, in the same way that police detectives might investigate a crime. But anyone studying the files can see that wasn't the case. Investigations seem to merely involve sending out a letter with a questionnaire to be filled out by the witness. The goal seemed to be to explain everything away in a tidy fashion. And if that couldn't be done, they marked the sighting as "unknown" and moved on.

Chapters 8, 9, and 10 in this book are Missouri unknown cases from the 1960s, the final decade that **Project Blue Book** was in operation.

8. A secret spy program?

RICHARDS-GEBAUER AFB, Missouri, (April 17, 1960, 8:29 p.m.) — Could it have been a visitor from outer space?

Was it meteor?

Or was it really one of ours — the re-entry of an early test flight of America's first reconnaissance satellite program, called Discoverer 11?

Whatever the red streaking object was that two Midwest astronomers watched on a cool dark night in the spring of 1960 south of Kansas City, it was unusual.

In fact, they were excited about it. One of them called it "extraordinary."

But what was it? Our government still has the sighting of the UFO they saw 57 years ago as of this writing listed among the 701 "unknowns" of **Project Blue Book's** case files.

Getting eyes in the sky

To understand the significance of such sightings as these, you have to go back to that particular time in history.

By 1960, the U.S. and the Soviet Union were deep in the most frigid part of the Cold War. It was a time when Americans were worried the U.S. had fallen behind in the space race — all because of a small beeping object about the size of a beach-ball.

The Soviets had launched the first artificial Earth satellite, Sputnik 1, on Oct. 4, 1957. Sputnik 2 followed on Nov. 3, 1957. It carried a 3-year-old stray dog, Laika — the first animal to orbit the Earth — who sadly died of overheating within a few hours after launch.

Meanwhile, the U.S. was trying to play catch-up to the Soviets.

The Sputnik launches had created a political crisis. Not only were the Soviets the first to successfully launch an orbiting satellite, the Sputnik program also showed that the Soviets could launch a missile with a nuclear warhead — and send it anywhere in the world.

Sputnik led to the U.S. stepping up its public space efforts. And just a few months after Sputnik, the Army's Explorer program placed the first American satellite into orbit, on Jan. 31, 1958.

However, the CIA's top secret U-2 program had already been clandestinely looking down from lower levels of space since July 1956.

Each of the cartographic images shot by U-2 pilots from about 70,000 feet covered 400 square miles of territory, capturing on film a treasure trove of data that could be analyzed and passed on to military leaders.

Back then, the U.S. did not acknowledge it had such "Angels" in the sky as the U-2.

However, the CIA has released statements in recent years saying that about half of the UFOs reported from that time period that were listed as unknowns could be attributed to U-2 aircraft.

Interestingly, the April 17, 1960, sighting at the Richards-Gebauer AFB was only about two weeks before the secret was out about the U-2s. CIA U-2 pilot Gary Powers would be shot down over Soviet airspace on May 1, 1960, which then blew the lid off the secret reconnaissance missions.

Spying from the heavens

Before Powers was shot down, the Soviet Sputnik launch had already spurred efforts to get the U.S. surveillance cameras into space.

By 1960, the Air Force had built and started testing its own cloak-and-dagger spy satellite system, called the Corona program.

The top-secret plan was to send up a small satellite with a sophisticated camera that could take images from earth orbit.

The clandestine satellite pod would re-enter the atmosphere, parachute down and be snatched in mid air — in slick 1960s-style James Bond fashion — by a military aircraft. Then the film would be safely spirited away to the newly created, super secret National Reconnaissance Office (NRO) for study.

At that time, the Corona program was hush-hush. But thanks to information about Corona that was declassified in 1995, we now know that the first Corona test flight had taken place on Feb. 28, 1959.

And the first successful mission, including the recovery of film, took place on Aug. 12, 1960. We also know now there were many test flights in between — including Discoverer 11, which launched on April 15, 1960. You have to pay close attention to the dates.

The Discovery launch was *only two days* before the two Kansas City astronomers saw something red streaking across the night sky on April 17 of that year — and those astronomers may have correctly guessed it was part the Discoverer program.

Disinformation from NASA

Although the real mission of the Discoverer program wasn't made public at that time, NASA did put out a cover story about the space launches.

NASA now admits that Discoverer *"was presented as a program to orbit large satellites to test satellite subsystems and investigate the communication and environmental aspects of placing humans in space, including carrying biological packages for return to Earth from orbit."*

(See https://nssdc.gsfc.nasa.gov/nmc/spacecraftDisplay.do?id=1960-004A)

That was actually a lie — a cover story — to hide the real reason for the Cold War spy rocket launches.

NASA now admits that what the secret Corona program was actually designed to do was to look in on the Soviets and their Chinese allies from space:

"The primary goal of the program was to develop a film-return photographic surveillance satellite to assess how rapidly the Soviet Union was producing long-range bombers and ballistic missiles and where they were being deployed, and to take photos over the Sino-Soviet bloc to replace the U2 spy planes."

According to NASA, one of those launches was two days before the Richards-Gebauer AFB sighting. Discoverer 11 was launched from Vandenberg AFB on April 15. It was orbiting every 92.16 minutes.

The exact date of the test to recover the film isn't specified in NASA's public notes on the project.

The NASA website says, *"The satellite used a film canister that was returned to earth in a capsule (a.k.a. bucket) for evaluation.*

These capsules were designed to be recovered by a specially equipped aircraft during parachute descent, but were also designed to float to permit recovery from the ocean. All film were black and white. Discoverer 11's film capsule recovery failed."

The history information website says that Discoverer 11's "decay date" was April 26, which indicates that's when it burned up upon re-entry.

What does that mean to the Richards-Gebauer unknown sighting?

It's possible that on April 17, 1960, what the two Kansas City astronomers saw was one of America's first efforts to bring the James Bond-style film buckets back to Earth.

The red streak they saw was possibly the film canister glowing red hot on re-entry.

An extraordinary sight

It's unclear how **Project Blue Book** came across this case.

What's in the case file is not a report to the military, but Air Force Major Jim Ford's memo on April 18, 1960, to the Smithsonian Visual Tracking Center in Cambridge, Mass.

The typed memo is titled in its subject line: "Sighting Report – Extraordinary."

Ford's memo explained he was outside with a fellow astronomer, A. Chapdelaine.

He and Chapdelaine had been viewing M-42, a bright nebula in the Orion constellation *"when this spectacle occurred."*

"We sensed we were seeing something extraordinary," Ford wrote.

Moonwatchers

What exactly were the two men up to, searching the skies on that night in April?

Although their memo didn't say so, we can guess they might have been part of a registered station of (or at least familiar with) the national "Moon Watch" program.

Ford's memo starts off by saying he was submitting his information after consulting with a man *"who heads the K.C. Moon Watch."*

What was Moon Watch?

The Smithsonian Astrophysical Observatory at Cambridge, Massachusetts, had set up the Moonwatch program in 1957.

It was a form of what would be called today, in the modern Internet age, as "crowdsourcing." The Moonwatch program was designed to gather information about the new American satellites that were to begin orbiting the earth by enlisting the eyes of many volunteer amateur astronomers throughout the country.

The idea was to have a backup plan to help keep watch on these miniature "moons" when the satellites' radios quit working or when the government's own large mega-telescopes lost track of them.

The volunteer amateurs, with their low-end "toy" telescopes, could be enlisted in an emergency to search 24-7 until the "moons" were hunted down.

Just before the Sputnik launch in October 1957, the magazine *Popular Science* had published a story in its September 1957 issue discussing the new Moonwatch stations and how they would be key in tracking the silvery 20-inch satellites after their radios had gone silent and their orbits had started to deteriorate.

At the time of that story, there were about 1,400 amateurs who had been enlisted at 84 different Project Moonwatch observing stations.

W. Patrick McCray's book, **Keep Watching the Skies!** about Operation Moonwatch puts the participation rate at 200 teams around the world, with more than half in the United States.

The stations organized teams of stargazers to "guard" a sector in the sky they had been assigned, with amateur telescopes placed closed together in an observing line to watch the dark skies after nightfall.

"We believe that these teams may well be recognized in the future as pioneers in the greatest scientific research project ever participated in by non-professional observers," J. Allen Hynek, who was in charge of the optical Satellite Tracking Program, told *Popular Science*. Hynek, as mentioned earlier in this book, was also **Project Blue Book's** go-to scientist whenever they had an unknown sighting — and at that time, Hynek was still a UFO debunker.

By the time of the Richard-Gebauers AFB sighting, Moonwatch had been gathering satellite reports for more than two years.

Ford's account

Major Jim Ford's memo to the Smithsonian's visual tracking center says his observation took place the evening of April 17, 1960.

He reports that the weather was fair and the temperature was 40 degrees.

They first spotted the moving object at 8:29 p.m. north of the belt in Orion at an estimated 30 degrees above the horizon. They saw it with unaided eyes and with their six-inch Newtonian 48x telescope, which had a one-inch eyepiece.

The object, which Ford reports had a reddish glow, was traveling in an arc toward the southwest. They watched it for 2.5 minutes as it passed 1 degree south of Sirius, falling below the horizon at 8:31:30 p.m.

The object subtended five seconds of arc and had *"an undetermined profile,"* Ford wrote.

"During sighting period there was no apparent change in either size, color, or magnitude. The angular rate of change of the object appeared to increase from 2 degrees per minute — estimated — in Orion to 1 degree per second at last sighting."

"The first 30 seconds we watched and debated the origin of the flight. This was no aircraft. Then we checked the object's track. At first we thought it to be a polar orbit — but on checking it with the celestial polar axis, an orbit near 45 degrees appeared more reasonable. In a desperate effort I got the object in the narrow field of my telescope. Unfortunately I did not get a good focus."

Then there was Ford's key question to the Smithsonian tracking center: *"Did we observe a vehicle of the Discoverer class on reentry just prior to its becoming a fire-ball?"*

Unfortunately, Ford probably never received a response — at least there is no responding letter contained in the **Project Blue Book** files.

It does appear someone from **Project Blue Book** did try to follow up on Ford's sighting.

A notation on the project record card for the incident says "Request for additional information sent and no answer received."

The *"Conclusions"* area on the record card has a typed *"X"* in the *"Unknown"* checkbox, including the word *"UNIDENTI-FIED."*

A note in the *"Comments"* area says, *"From the information given no conclusion can be offered. Case listed as unidentified."*

However, did Major Ford correctly identify that red streak in the sky?

Based on what we now know from declassified information that was released decades later, that's entirely likely.

Ford's sighting might have been the first of many such secret unidentified reconnaissance satellites that are still being placed into orbit by the CIA, the Air Force and the Navy.

We know now, thanks to documents that were declassified in 1995, that later in 1960 a new clandestine agency was established to oversee all of the spy satellites being launched by the CIA and the military.

That agency, called the National Reconnaissance Office, was finally made known to the public in 1985. And the NRO, called the country's ears and eyes in space, is still working on secret space projects.

The Washington Post estimated its budget at $10.3 billion for 2013 in "black projects."

(See http://www.washingtonpost.com/wp-srv/special/national/black-budget/)

Although this chapter's sighting probably has an explanation, the sighting in the next chapter seems like something out of science fiction.

9. **Burning red orb**

ST. LOUIS, Missouri (8:30 p.m. July 19, 1960) — A meteor doesn't fly overhead, stop, and then go in the opposite direction. A star doesn't. Neither does a planet.

So what is that thing? Is it one of ours? Is it Russian? Or could it be something else, something not from this world?

The red, glowing orb showed up just before dusk on a summer evening nearly six decades ago over St. Louis.

Some people were outside, enjoying the cool evening weather after a hot day. They were talking, or watching the fireflies and the stars pop out just at the edge of nightfall. Some were indoors, catching an evening black-and-white network TV program, such as the "Adventures of Ozzie and Harriet," "Hawaiian Eye" or "Men into Space."

But there was something different out there that evening in the sky — a strange red object that was behaving peculiarly. The object's movements had attracted the attention of T. L. Ochs and at least two others. Ochs started watching it closely, wondering what it was.

Then it was gone.

UFO returns

Ochs happened to be looking up outside the next night, July 20, 1960, when strangely, the red object reappeared and resumed its peculiar activity. Strangely enough, the red object came back again a third night, July 21, 1960, giving another remarkable, but worrisome performance.

It's likely that if Ochs had seen the object today, he probably would have pulled out a cell phone camera and taken a video or photo. We would have been able to listen to him describe it in wonder as it darted around the sky. He might have posted it on Twitter, on Facebook or Instagram. He might have notified his local MUFON chapter.

But back in the 1960s, people were less likely to have the equipment to film or photograph such remarkable occurrences.

However, they also thought a little differently about UFOs than we do today. They felt more compelled to go to the authorities to report it and to find answers — even directly to the president of the United States, if they were compelled enough to do so.

Ochs reported the sightings to authorities. We don't know exactly what questions he asked. But we can guess.

Was it ours — something secret being tested by the CIA or the military? Could it have been a Soviet reconnaissance aircraft or spacecraft? Or was it something else? An alien spacecraft like in science fiction novels or movies?

But the military's UFO investigators couldn't explain it either — or at least they weren't saying.

So the red orb over St. Louis remains on the books as one of the U.S. Air Force **Project Blue Book's** 701 "unknowns."

Larger than the moon?

There are 12 documents in **Project Blue Book's** archives on the mysterious red orb's multiple sightings, which took place at various times of the evenings of July 19, 20 and 21, 1960, over the skies of St. Louis.

The *Project 10073 Record Card* says the object was watched from the ground for 20- and 30-minute periods during each of the episodes.

The record card's summary says the object was round, "about the size of a quarter." At that time, UFO investigators had devised a simple system of measuring the size of an unidentified flying object by having the witness explain its size in relationship to the comparative size of a common object held at arm's length.

So from this description — the size of a quarter — we can guess that the object was much larger in the sky than the moon. A full moon would be smaller than the size of a U.S. dime held at arm's length.

Or, perhaps, Ochs was merely over-estimating its size.

The summary on the record card says the round object was *"bright red with varying intensity, first seen overhead, last seen E* [east] *at high altitude."*

The record card says the object stopped, hovered and went backward once or twice. The first night the object disappeared to the east after 20 minutes. The second night it disappeared to the west after 30 minutes.

Dear President Eisenhower ...

Ochs wasn't the only one reporting it.

We do know that at the time of the writing, some of Ladue's citizens were fairly well-to-do and highly educated — it was a suburb where many people in the St. Louis area with higher incomes lived.

Census reports show that Ladue had about 9,400 people at the time, compared to about 8,500 now. It had also been home to George Herbert Walker, who went on to be a Wall Street banker, and whose grandson, George H. W. Bush, and great-grandson, George W. Bush, went on to be U.S. presidents.

Often, if someone has money, their business or social connections include prominent people in power in Washington, D.C.

So it makes sense that one of the documents in the files is a written correspondence from a Ladue witness to President Dwight D. Eisenhower, who then was in the middle of his second term.

The two-page letter, written in perfect cursive, is from one of several witnesses who had probably been discussing the sighting. Except for "Mrs.," most of the signature at the bottom of the letter has been blotted out on the document in the archive.

Dated July 20, 1960, the letter to President Eisenhower takes us right back to the second night of the sightings. The descriptions are concise and precise, suggesting the writer had a strong command of language and was accustomed to putting her thoughts down on paper.

In this case, the woman appears to have known the president well enough to pen him a letter — or bold enough to just go right to the top to seek answers.

"One hour ago, at 9:50 p.m., I witnessed a very strange event in the sky north of my St. Louis County home," she writes.

"A red object shining with extreme intensity appeared traveling slowly from NE to NW. It rose sharply and then disappeared at 10:03 pm. as one would turn off an electric light bulb. This strange occurrence was also witnessed by many people last night in St. Louis County. It is fearful to see such a thing."

The tone of the woman's letter was one of frustration.

At the end of her letter, she indicated that she knew she saw something — and somebody should be able to tell her what was going on.

However, her letter indicated that no St. Louis-area authorities, including the weather bureau, the police or local newspapers, have been able to give her an adequate explanation.

"Weather balloons and satellites have been ruled out," she wrote.

"It was shining too brightly for a balloon and was too low for a satellite.

"I am positive there is a logical cause for the strange sight I witnessed this evening. If the explanation is classified information cannot some prominent authority at least put our minds at ease and say 'don't worry just forget it.'"

Not an aircraft

It seems that the woman's letter to the president worked — it brought a fairly quick response.

The **Blue Book** files show the woman received a response letter dated July 29, 1960, from USAF Lt. Col. Lawrence J. Tacker, of the Public Information Division, Office of Information.

"Your letter dated 20 July 1960 concerning an unidentified flying object and addressed to President Eisenhower has been referred to this office," Tacker wrote. *"Your letter contains insufficient information for a valid conclusion. Therefore I am inclosing a U.S. Air Force questionnaire, which should be filled out and sent to the Aerospace Technical Intelligence Center at Wright-Patterson Air Force Base, Ohio, for their analysis and evaluation.*

"For your information I am inclosing the latest Department of Defense fact sheet which plainly states the Air Force's position regarding UFOs."

'Burning bright red'

The documents in the case file include *ATIC Form No. 164*, the official Air Force questionnaire Mrs. [REDACTED] filled out in cursive on Aug. 1, 1960.

On Page 1, we learn she first spotted it at approximately 9:50 p.m. July 20, 1960, and watched it from the back yard of her home in Ladue.

According to the USAF questionnaire, the object was visible for 10 to 15 minutes — and she circled *"certain"* about that length of time. For the condition of the sky, she circled the response *"No trace of daylight."*

On the next page, she circled that there were *"Many stars"* in the sky, but she didn't remember if she saw the moon.

She circled *"Yes"* that the object was brighter than the background of the sky.

The next question asked if the brightness she saw was like that of an automobile headlight.

"No, much more bright." She underlined *"much more."* She also circled a response that it looked similar to a headlight that was *"a mile or more away (a distant car)?"* Next to her answer, she penned *"probably less [distance] — Hard to say."*

The questionnaire then covered the UFO's movements.

She circled *"Yes"* that it appeared to stand still at any time, that it changed in brightness, and that it flickered, throbbed, or pulsated.

She circled *"No"* that it did not suddenly speed up and rush away at any time, that it didn't break up into parts or explode, that it didn't give off smoke, and that it didn't change shape.

She circled *"No"* that the object didn't move behind or in front of anything, including a cloud. Asked how the object appeared, she circled both *"Solid"* and *"Don't know."*

Was she looking at the object through eyeglasses, window glass, a windshield, binoculars, telescope, theodolite or anything else? She responded *"nothing."*

Another question asked what she heard — *"No sound."* Another question asked her to describe the color — *"Burning bright red."*

Red lines emanate

The questionnaire contained a blank space for her to draw a picture of what it looked like in the sky, labeling any details, such as wings, protrusions, exhaust or vapor trails and to use arrows to show the direction.

Her sketch has an "N" at the top for north, an "S" at the bottom for south, a "W" on the left for west and an "E" on the right for east.

At the upper right is an arrow pointed to the west.

Slightly off-centered to the left she put the UFO — she drew a round dark circle, colored in with ink.

And then she put in something very strange she hadn't mentioned before — six long wavy rays coming out from the UFO.

To the right of her drawing she wrote in cursive: *"Burning bright nucleus about size of a baseball. Actually saw lines that appeared to be caused by the burning of the center. Nothing else was seen."*

On the next question, she circled an answer that the object's edges were *"Like a bright star."*

Next to that answer she wrote *"Nucleus was like a burning red solid. Then long red lines emanated out from 'solid' part."*

The next question directed her to draw a picture to show the motion of the object, placing an "A" at the beginning of the path and a "B" at the end, showing any changes in direction.

Her drawing shows the object started traveling down and to the west, then up into the sky. She shows that by drawing a dashed line moving down at about a 30-degree angle, then moving up at 90 degrees, writing *"(going straight up)."*

Below the UFO, she drew a tree, a dot representing where she stood, and rectangles showing her house and her back porch.

Unsure of dimensions

The next question asked her to try to guess or estimate the real size of the object in its longest dimension in feet.

She wrote *"6 inches perhaps. I really couldn't tell how high it was, so it's a guess."*

The next question asked specifically how large it was as compared with one of the following objects held in the hand and at about arm's length: head of a pin, pea, dime, nickel, quarter, half dollar, silver dollar, baseball, grapefruit, basketball or other. She circled *"Baseball."*

How certain was she of the size? She circled *"Not very sure."* And she penned in *"Could have been larger."*

Next, she was asked how the object disappeared from view.

"It rose slowly in the sky toward the big dipper. It then went 'out' suddenly, as you would turn off an electric light."

She was then asked to compare it to a common object that might give the same appearance.

"The object I saw was burning brightly perhaps like a flare but it did not light up the sky as a flare would. The nucleus was solid appearing, and it seemed to pulsate or flicker but actually never went out. The redness and the burning were the 2 outstanding characteristics. It moved slowly and seemed in the beginning low in the sky. I can't describe it in terms of anything I ever saw before."

The 25th question on the form asked her where she was — *"On my back porch when I first spotted it."* She also circled that she was in the residential section of the city.

She ran outside

Question 27 asked what she was doing at the time and how did she happen to notice it.

Her answer revealed how startling it was — enough to get her to rush outdoors to look at it.

"I was watching T.V. It was out of the corner of my eye that I no-ticed something bright red in the sky," she wrote. *"I ran outside then."*

She circled she was looking north when she first saw it. And when she last saw the UFO, she was looking *"straight up, but slightly northwest."*

Asked about the weather conditions, she circled that there was a clear sky, no wind, dry condition, and a warm temperature.

Asked if anyone else was with her when she saw it, she responded, yes, that her husband was with her and yes, he saw it too.

She had written his name on the questionnaire, but it has been blotted out.

Was this the first time that you had seen an object or objects like this? She circled *"yes."*

Asked what she thought it was and what might have caused it, she wrote *"I have not the slightest idea. Neither does my hus-band."*

The form asked her if she could estimate the UFO's speed in miles per hour. She circled *"no,"* writing to the side *"It only seemed to be moving slowly."*

How far away was she? *"Perhaps a ½ mile or less,"* she wrote.

Husband's first name was Bob

At the end of the questionnaire, there was a lined page for her to write in more details.

She apparently was concerned they might not take her word for it. So she put in some information about her husband to show his integrity.

"(My husband is a college graduate and has seen service in 2 wars as an officer. He was in combat during the Korean war.)"

She then began a narrative of what happened.

*"When I spotted this object we were both watching T.V. My hus-*band, [his name is blotted out], *was in the house; I was on the porch on a chair. I ran outside and yelled for* [name redacted] *to come quickly.*

"We saw the object move slowly across the sky until it was just 'above' our sycamore tree and then it seemed to hover and seemed very close. It was burning and flickering to a great degree. It pulsat-ed and seemed to get brighter, darker, brighter, darker (I said this to myself when I saw it).

"It always remained a brilliant red. I was stunned and glued to the spot. Bob [here her husband's name was not redacted) *rushed to the phone at this point and called the Ladue police to make a re-port. They said that they had a radio report from the County police already.* [**Bob's** name is redacted] *ran back outside. In the mean-time I had not taken my eye off of the object. It started to move high-er in the sky.*

"It became much smaller — merely a small red light.

"In the vicinity of the big dipper, it went <u>out</u> [she underlined out].

"Bob [his name was not removed here] *saw this happen too. We ran into the kitchen and saw the time was 10:05 p.m. We estimated we had seen the object from ten to fifteen minutes.*

"Our deepest anxiety for the next several hours was not the danger of the object we had seen but the fact that neither of us could identify it as anything we had ever seen before.

"We decided to make a report to someone who could use information on this sort of thing or someone who could tell us what it was.

"We called the weather bureau ... [her writing here is indecipherable because of a dark online photocopy]. *We called the two daily newspapers. They had received many calls about the object and could not identify it. We called the F.B.I.* [indecipherable] *... call Air Field and ...* [indecipherable] *to file a report. I decided to also write the president knowing my letter would be referred to a concerned party. This letter to him was written about an hour after seeing the object. We had been constantly on the phone up until then."*

She underlines each of her words in this sentence: *"If you can tell us what we saw last July 20, then we would appreciate your letting us know. Thank you Mrs.* [blotted out]."

If the Air Force did know, they weren't telling.

Even the official **Project Blue Book** analyst seemed stumped in his written assessment in the comments box on the official record

"The most probable cause of this sighting is high-flying a/c (aircraft). However, if the statement by the witness that the object hover is to be accepted this possibility must be ruled out (other than helicopters).

"This case is classed "Unidentified" for lack of data which points conclusively toward a solution."

And the woman, who would be about 87 years old as of this writing, and her husband, Bob, apparently never got their answer.

Answers are also still out there, somewhere, about the cold case I cover in the next chapter. Did the witness see a helicopter, a new type of military aircraft — or possibly an alien craft that was abducting his cattle?

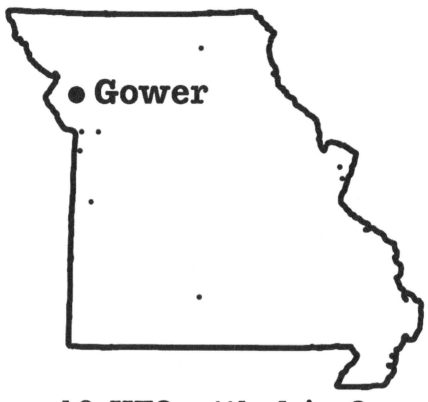

10. **UFO cattle drive?**

GOWER, Missouri, (Feb. 9, 1968) — When cows become up-set, they do more than moo. They cry and bellow. They moan. They snort and grunt.

Such cries of distress were coming from several dozen cattle pastured at a rural residence about 30 miles north of Kansas City, Missouri.

The cows' frantic cries woke up their 57-year-old owner. He sprang out of bed. Was somebody out there on this February morning? Could it be coyotes?

The man also heard another noise he couldn't quite place.

It was a pulsating wire-whipping sound that eerily cut through the pre-dawn winter stillness.

Peering out his living room window, he saw a huge aircraft hovering over his property, shining down yellowish green lights on his frightened animals.

Was this why he had been missing some cattle?

Still unexplained nearly 50 years later, the Missouri witness's story has been revisited by some of the top non-governmental UFO investigators in the world. His sighting has been featured in UFO books and on some websites.

No, the witness didn't actually see any of his bawling cattle being raised up into the night sky, like the cartoons that show cows being tractor-beamed into a flying saucer.

But what this Missouri cattleman did see and hear caught the attention of the Air Force's investigation into UFOs, **Project Blue Book,** where his sighting still remains as one of the last of the 701 official "unknowns" — a real-life X-File.

Detailed narrative

Unfortunately, the man's name has been blotted out in the **Blue Book** documents now kept in the National Archive in Washington, D.C.

He requested anonymity, which probably gave his story a little more plausibility and credibility to investigators.

His wish for privacy indicated he wanted to get answers for himself and possibly to notify authorities out of a sense of duty to the country and to his community.

They also show he didn't want his neighbors to label him as a UFO kook and diminish his standing in the community — and perhaps even put his job at risk.

The witness didn't bother calling local public officials. He went right to the top — to President's Lyndon B. Johnson's inner circle. He sent a letter the very next day to Secretary of Defense Robert F. McNamara in the Pentagon.

The heading at the top of his letter says *"Re: U. F. O."*

"Dear Sir:

"I reside on a farm approximately 30 miles north of Kansas City, Missouri. The residence is approximately ¼ mile back from the highway with a pasture in front of the dwelling. I am employed in town and operate a cow herd on an all-grass farm. If there is a disturbance among my cattle, I arise to their bawling as would a mother to her crying child.

"Last night I heard several cows bawl as though frightened or scared. I immediately jumped from my bed and ran to the picture window in my living room.

It was a dark night but there was a distinct glow giving off considerable light immediately in front of the house (approximately 300 to 350 feet away).

It made sufficient light for me to maneuver around a card table left in the middle of the room, and to see cattle in the pasture in a rough semi-circle to the left of the light glow.

*"**As my vision adjusted** from darkness to this moderate light, I was able to see parts of what appeared to be a tremendous circular object, reproduced as best I can on the attached sketch.*

"The light was a yellowish green and came from the concave sides of the craft. I could not tell whether it came from a translucent surface or was reflected from the base of the craft against a shiny surface and then back to the ground. In any event, there was sufficient light to see the major limbs on some walnut trees, a stump, the cows, fence in the foreground and other details.

'Monstrous helicopter'

The man's letter continues:

"The object appeared to be at least 100 feet in diameter, and to be hovering 20 to 23 feet above the ground . . . although I could not say that it was not on the ground, or possibly higher in the air.

"There were definitely seven openings or portholes in the approximate center of the concave sides. Their spacing would indicate that, if the craft were in fact round, there were probably 16 of these equally spaced around the craft. I could not see distinctly enough to tell if they were square, rectangular, oval or round. It was difficult to arrive at a perspective to judge their size but I would 'guess' they were two feet to 30 inches in approximate diameter. I saw no door or distinct opening.

"I saw no living thing enter or depart the craft. I have no idea whether I watched half a minute or five minutes, I was so entranced by the sight.

"I have been losing a cow or two now and then, undoubtedly stolen, without a trace.

"My first reaction, on hearing the cows, was that someone was among them. On seeing the craft, I remember thinking 'No wonder I have found no evidence. They are being hauled off by air.' At that moment I had no thought of what I saw being a possible U.F.O, but rather some monstrous helicopter or other craft.

*"**Some of the cows** were staring at this object from perhaps 100 to 200 feet away. Cows with younger calves were bawling, and some of the calves were answering. Finally one cow whirled and ran, with tail high, toward the barn. The others followed and in only a few seconds there were no cattle in sight. The craft remained some little time after the cows departed, but I have no idea whether this was half a minute or considerably longer. It was during this time that I concentrated on the object in an attempt to make out all the details I could."*

Pulsating sound

The man's letter mentions the eerie sounds coming from the craft.

"All during this time there had been a distinct noise that I have difficulty in describing. It sounded something like the swish of a piece of wire which one might whirl around above his head at high speed, and yet it had pulsating rhythm of some kind.

*"**When the craft departed**, this noise was two or three times louder and the sound pulsations were more rapid. The craft moved away rapidly toward the Southwest, arising at about a 45-degree angle without the craft being tilted in any way from the horizontal position it had maintained at, or above, ground level."*

A physical effect?

"When this brief experience was over I had hot flashes and felt chilled at the same time, and was perspiring all over.

"I went back to the bedroom and was surprised that my wife had not awakened.

"I then recalled I had not seen my dog or heard him bark although he is usually quite alert to any disturbance.

A normal evening

"I am 57 years of age, employed as [redacted] for Panhandle Eastern Pipe Line Company in Kansas City, Missouri, and of sober habits.

Last night I had attended the County Planning and Zoning Commission meeting, of which I [redacted]. I came home about a quarter to ten, watched the news on T-V and retired.

Mrs. [redacted] was away at an AAUW meeting, came home later, bathed and retired without awakening me.

When I returned to the bedroom, after the experience related in the above paragraphs, it was 4:35. I must have been awakened sometime between 4:20 and 4:30.

"More I cannot tell you. I have made no announcement to anyone in the local area. I certainly seek no notoriety or publicity of any kind. If I can be of any assistance to any one who is seriously investigating this kind of report, I will be pleased to cooperate on a 'no publicity' basis."

His signature was redacted.

But those who tried to give him anonymity forgot to cross out the initials at the bottom: *"RWB/vb."*

That's a standard office reference for the years prior to desktop computers that means R.W.B. wrote the letter and then gave it to V.B., who polished it up and typed it into a formal letter with attachments.

V.B. was most likely his wife or a personal secretary, considering he wanted no publicity — and he told a **Project Blue Book** investigator that except for his letter to McNamara, he had told no one but his wife about the incident.

What else could it be?

What's especially interesting about R.W.B.'s sighting is that he describes it as saucer-shaped — but he also sketches something a little different.

R.W.B. provided two drawings with his letter to the Secretary of Defense. One was from his perspective from inside his house looking out his living picture room window, and a second sketch from a perspective looking down on his property, which showed where the craft was in relationship to his home.

What was very interesting was that the first drawing shows what appears to be a long fuselage with several portholes. As he drew it, there were lights coming from each side of this fuselage.

Without reading any more of the report, I guessed correctly what the UFO investigators must have thought — a helicopter.

A Chinook?

I found several photos on various websites of the Chinook helicopters, which had been developed in the early 1960s by Boeing. About 160 of the Chinooks had been ordered in 1966 by the Army to be used in the Vietnam War for moving troops and heavy equipment.

What sets the Chinooks apart from other helicopters is that they have twin rotors, a long fuselage and several portholes across the fuselage — similar to the portholes in the witness' sketch. The Chinook fuselage is also angled in the rear, which seemed to match up with the sketch that the man drew.

I was about ready to write off this UFO siting as a Chinook until I saw the dimensions R.W.B. had precisely drawn on his sketch.

While today's Chinooks can be almost 100 feet in length, the Chinooks the military was using in 1968 were only about half the size of the craft in his sketch.

The specs on the CH-47 medium helicopters used at the time show they were 51 feet long, 10 feet six inches wide with a rotor diameter of 59 feet, 1.25 inches. R.W.B.'s meticulous drawing indicated the craft he saw was 100 feet in diameter.

And, as R.W.B. indicated on his drawing from the top perspective, the craft he saw was round. Also, the two spinning rotor blades of the Chinook probably did not make the wire whipping sound he was hearing.

So if what he saw was indeed a Chinook, it would have been twice the size of any helicopters that were being developed at that time by Boeing.

Could this have been a specially made Chinook?

If so, it didn't make any sense that they would be testing it in overnight darkness secretly above a herd of cattle 30 miles north of Kansas City, Missouri.

And why would Boeing or the military be hiding something that big? Could it have been a special aircraft ordered by the CIA?

Limited response

Like some people who made reports at the time, R.W.B. got a written response. It came a week later, dated Feb. 16, 1968, from Lt. Col. David L. Stiles, who was a chief information officer assigned to the case by the Secretary of the Air Force.

Stiles wrote: *"Without additional information, we cannot offer an explanation of the unidentified flying object (UFO) you observed. However, if you will complete the attached questionnaire and mail it in the enclosed envelope, our technical people at Wright-Patterson Air Force Base will be able to investigate further and make an evaluation."*

The next paragraph seemed a little like R.W.B. was being chastised for going to the Secretary of Defense.

"Should you ever sight another UFO, please report it as soon as possible to the nearest Air Force base. Each base has a UFO investigator, who is in a better position to make an on-the-spot investigation, which usually results in a more accurate analysis."

"In the meantime, we are sending you some literature that may help you identify your sighting. Thank you for reporting it to the Air Force."

As far as we know, R.W.B. didn't respond to Stiles' letter. He must have thought he had done his duty and it was obvious the Air Force wasn't going to pursue it further.

Hynek personally investigated

However, the Air Force did pursue it.

One of the interesting aspects of this case is that J. Allen Hynek, the Air Force's longtime scientific consultant of the UFO phenomenon, was called upon to personally interview the witness.

At the time, Hynek was director of the Lindheimer Astronomical Research Center in the Department of Astronomy at Northwestern University. He had been called upon regularly as a consultant to **Project Blue Book** since its early days.

The files contain a two-page typed and signed memo that Hynek sent to **Project Blue Book's** director, Major Hector Quintanilla Jr., who was chief of the Aerial Phenomena office of the Foreign Technology division of the Air Force headquarters at the Wright Patterson base in Dayton, Ohio.

Hynek's written evaluation is a response to a short memo that Quintanilla sent him on March 26 (more than six weeks after the sighting) requesting that he contact the witness.

Hynek explains that when he first contacted the witness by telephone, the witness was in the hospital with a kidney stone. So Hynek talked to the man's wife, who did not experience the sighting.

"I wanted to evaluate her manner of speaking and thinking. The conversation revealed that she is a matter-of-fact, down-to-earth individual who has lived in that community all her life," Hynek wrote to Quintanilla

The couple owned their own farm and raised registered cattle for breeding purposes, Hynek wrote.

"Nothing in my conversation with Mrs. [redacted] would indicate that she is excitable or any other than a common sense person."

Hynek's memo says that the following day he telephoned R.W.B. at the hospital and had an extended talk with him.

"No other significant facts concerning the sighting itself emerged from the conversation," Hynek wrote. *"His letter, as you note, was articulate and concise and covered the basic facts. Mr. [redacted] does not wish to fill out our questionnaire. He feels that little could be added, and he pointed out that he nearly didn't write his letter in the first place, but did so only because he felt the matter might be of some interest to the government.*

"I questioned him on such matters as duration, angular sizes, acceleration, and trajectory. The object did not pass in front of any object, but he thought it may have passed somewhat behind two walnut trees.

"He stated that it had been completely stationary close to the ground for about ten times as long as the duration of takeoff and disappearance."

Hynek seemed to think that the witness was telling the truth about what he saw.

"Mr. [redacted]'s whole manner of speech was careful and he made no attempt to embellish his story, or to do anything other than stick to the facts.

"He does not desire publicity and has not mentioned the incident to anyone other than his wife. He feels no good could come from talking about it. I would have to give Mr. [redacted] a very good rating as to stability and unexcitability."

But there was one thing that Hynek saw as a possible problem — the witness' eyesight. The man's letter had indicated he didn't have his glasses on at the time.

"He is, however, nearsighted and although he tells me he can drive without glasses, he rarely does," Hynek wrote. *"Had he had his glasses on, he feels he could have observed more details than he did."*

Conclusion: Unknown

Hynek wrote that the case *"must be evaluated as underlined,"* underlining the word in his memo.

"Since it is a one-witness case (if we exclude the cows as witnesses) we are up the familiar blind alley with the question as to whether there was an actual image on Mr. [redacted]'s retina at the time of his sighting. There is always the possibility that this could have been a vivid dream or an outright hallucination. We do not understand under what conditions such hallucinations occur but in my recent visit in London I spoke at great length with a well-know psychiatrist who is doing research in hypnosis and he tells me the following:

"One out of 20 people appear to be capable of deep trance hypnosis. In some five cases in which he had hypnotized the people who have spectacular UFO sightings he has found that in all cases these people were capable of deep trance hypnosis.

Deep trance subjects are capable of hallucination under suggestion by the hypnotist. The question remains whether they are also capable of hallucination without the aid of a hypnotist. This is an interesting possibility and might go a long way toward explaining many of the single witness cases."

Hynek wrote that he questioned the witness as to whether he had ever been hypnotized. The man told him that he never had and that *"sort of stuff was out of his field."*

In Hynek's memo, someone has hand-underlined part of Hynek's next paragraph (it might have been Hynek or Quintanilla) as follows:

"If we do not accept hallucination, and there is no a priori reason to accept it, we are faced with the generally unpalatable conclusion that Mr. [redacted] did indeed see what he said he saw.

"I find no ordinary artifact, weather conditions, aircraft, or mirage, etc., which would serve to explain this sighting," Hynek wrote in conclusion.

In his book, the *Hynek UFO Report* (Page 195), Hynek explains what happened after he sent in his analysis to Quintanilla — **Blue Book's** director decided not to do a follow-up face-to-face interview with the witness.

Such interviews are important because they might draw out more information that would be useful, Hynek wrote.

*"**Blue Book** simply stuck on a label, [unidentified] and considered the case closed."*

Two more witnesses emerge

The Groveton file contains a second letter that could verify R.W.B.'s sighting. However, the two witnesses didn't actually see a UFO — they heard one.

The letter, postmarked April 23, 1968, was sent about six weeks after the sighting to Quintanilla, **Blue Book's** director.

Most of the sender's name has been blotted out. However, "Mrs." is still visible in her signature, along with a partial address of Kansas City, Missouri.

Sounds were 'exactly the same'

"Dear Major Quintanilla,

"I am enclosing an article which appeared in our Kansas City Star, on April 23, 1968. I was very interested because sometime during February, both my daughter and I heard the same kind of noise.

"I was awakened one night about 2:30, by this sound. Please under-stand I am not [she underlined several words for emphasis] a flying saucer buff. I am very interested and neither believe nor disbelieve but have an open mind. I have never heard a sound to compare with this, and interestingly enough, half awake and rushing to the window, my first thought was 'UFO' — I could see nothing, but my description of the sound is exactly the same as the one quoted in the article.

"My daughter, who is 22, heard the same sound several nights later but by the time she awaked me, I could only hear it faintly, receding into the distance.

"We mentioned this to some friends who told us perhaps this was a new device the police were occasionally using on their cars. We were finally able to hear this, and tho similar to some degree, it was not the same thing by any means.

'Roughly speaking, I think we heard these noises about the middle of February.

'I had to write you, because I was actually dumfounded to read such a literal description of what I too, had heard, but not seen."

She enclosed a short, one-column newspaper clipping that was headlined "For More on UFO" with a subhead, "Air Force Asks St. Joseph, Mo., Official for Report."

The Associated Press story, with a dateline of St. Joseph, Mo., said that Quintanilla had asked John C. Riley Jr., city aviation director, for information about "a reported unidentified flying object in the Gower, Mo., area a 4:30 o'clock in the morning, February 9."

The story included a few sentences from Quintanilla's written request: *"The observer sighted an extremely bright light and also heard a noise. It sounded similar to the swish of a piece of wire, whirled at high speed above a person's head, and had pulsating rhythm of some kind. Initially, the object was hovering, but when it moved toward the southwest, the noise was two or three times louder and the sound pulsations were more rapid."*

Director seeks answers

The **Blue Book** file on R.W.B.'s sighting showed that Quintanilla had made several other inquiries. His later memos give the location as Gower, Missouri, rather than "Groveton."

Although the director was a skeptic of any extraterrestrial explanation of UFOs, the memos show he was at least looking into the case for a conventional explanation.

Besides writing to the St. Joseph, Mo., city aviation director, the **Blue Book** files also indicate the director sent memos on April 17, 1968, to the police departments and airports in the Kansas City area and in northwest Missouri.

The file includes written responses to the memo from a few officials.

Lt. Gaylord Mayer, commanding officer of the records and identification unit for the Kansas City, Missouri, Police Department, wrote that the department had not received a written or verbal report of the Feb. 9, 1968, UFO observation.

"Since Gower, Missouri is located near the TWA Overhaul Base, north of Kansas City, Mo., it could be assumed that the activities at the base would have a bearing, what may have caused this unusual report. We regret not being able to assist you in this matter."

Kenneth A. Corn, police clerk for Plattsburgh, Missouri, wrote: *"I have no information on any such sighting."*

Emerson S. Capps, tower chief at the Mid Continent International Airport in Kansas City, Missouri, responded *"No helicopters are based or operate from here. No reports were received from controllers in the tower."*

James R. Kennedy, facility chief at the Kansas City Municipal Airport, on April 23, 1968, wrote *"Except for unusual incidents, we have disposed of our aircraft movement records for the concerned date. No incident similar to the UFO observation was recorded at the control tower.*

"Helicopter operations from this airport normally do not operate in the area or at the time involved.

"The observations related in paragraph 2 of your memorandum give indications of low altitude operation of a turbine-powered helicopter. I would suggest contacting Sherman AAF, Fort Leavenworth, Kansas, and Marshall AAF, Fort Riley, Kansas, for possible information. Those facilities are both southwest of the location reported and conduct extensive helicopter operations."

During the time that Quintanilla was seeking answers to the mysterious sighting over Missouri, the **Blue Book** director had gone up in rank from a major to a lieutenant colonel.

By the time he sent a memo April 29, 1968, to the Marshall AAF at Fort Riley, Kansas, he signed his name with his new rank.

In that April 29 memo, Lt. Col. Quintanilla provides the same details about the bright light and the whirling wire sounds R.W.B. saw and heard on Feb. 9.

"Mr. [redacted], *Facility Chief at the Kansas City Municipal Airport, has suggested that the sighting may have been of a low altitude operation of a turbine-powered helicopter and suggested that we contact you.*

"Do helicopters from your field ever operate in the area in question? Do you have records for the above date and time that would indicate whether a helicopter or other aircraft would be in the area at the time? If so, was there any activity in the area at that time."

Quintanilla noted that he realized there would be a bit of research involved, *"however, we would sincerely appreciate your answering these questions."*

The Groveton sighting files have a response dated April 24, 1968, from Lt. Col. John P. Westphal, aviation officer, at Fort Leavenworth's Sherman Army Airfield — no, it wasn't one of theirs.

Westphal writes, *"The description of the sighting does resemble, in an intangible way, the manner in which members of the laity describe our helicopters. However, our helicopters seldom operate in the vicinity of Gower, Missouri. More specifically, our records reveal no helicopter flights on 9 February 1968.*

"Sherman Army Airfield Control Tower is non-operational during the period 2300 to 0700 hours, therefore, it was not in a position to receive any reports of unusual objects or noise. The airfield operations office is open on a 24 hour basis and no report pertinent to the alleged sighting was received."

Major John R. Dickinson, post aviation officer, at Fort Riley replied to Quintanilla on May 3, 1968 — their Army helicopters hadn't been around R.W.B.'s ranch.

"A check of our aircraft operations indicates that no aircraft operating from Marshall Army Airfield were flown in or around the area of Gower, Missouri, on 9 February 1968.

"Our normal helicopter low level training is restricted to an area in the immediate vicinity of Fort Riley and Smokey Hill Bomb Range, Salina, Kansas.

"The area around Gower, Missouri, is not used by this post for helicopter training or flight missions. We do, on occasion, use the instrument landing facilities at Rosecrans Memorial, Saint Joseph, Missouri. However, no assigned aircraft operated at Rosecrans Memorial on 9 February 1968."

Groveton or Gower?

The **Blue Book** case file for R.W.B.'s northwest Missouri incident has more in it than most files. There are 25 pages of documents, which include typed and handwritten letters and memos, sketches and newspaper clippings.

However, a problem with the file is in the location of the sighting.

The official case file labels it as happening in "Groveton" Missouri. Several early official letters refer to it as happening in "Groveton." But there is no Groveton on Missouri's map, nor listed in any historical directory of Missouri towns, hamlets or villages.

R.W.B.'s letter says he lived about 30 miles north of Kansas City, Mo., which would be near Gower, a town directly on the border of Buchanan and Clinton counties.

Later in the files, there are documents that do say the event happened near Gower, including the short newspaper story.

Did **Blue Book's** director get Gower mixed up with another town, perhaps Groveton, Texas?

More than a month after the sighting, a memo the director wrote to Hynek referred to R.W.B.'s sighting as having occurred on "8 February 1968" (not Feb. 9), and saying he was "of Groveton, Missouri, Conservation Acres Ranch." Was Groveton the name R.W.B. gave to his ranch? The stationery R.W.B. used had some print at the top that was redacted to ensure his privacy, so it might have been the name of the ranch.

The following month, memos the director sent out to law enforcement and aviation authorities all referred to the location as Gower.

However, once the location was corrected to Gower, why did it continue to be filed under "Groveton?" Was the director just sloppy?

Was he merely going through the motions on this investigation? Was he following orders? Was this an attempt to misfile it?

Project Blue Book was actually in its final few years at the time of the sighting. For years, there had been an effort going on within the Air Force brass to shut it down.

Blue Book had many critics inside and outside of government, including vocal private UFO researchers who complained that the Air Force was doing a shoddy job and wanted the investigations to take a more scientific, professional approach, while others insisted UFOs were hogwash and a waste of time.

Many UFO researchers say that in **Project Blue Book's** later years — at the time of this sighting — the UFO investigation program was at best a public relations operation and at worst used as a disinformation campaign by the CIA.

R.W.B.'s case clearly shows there wasn't a great deal of effort being put into investigations. Despite the implications that a 100-foot ship was zipping around silently in the Midwest and might pose a threat to national security — or at the least be rustling cattle — the file indicates it was a fairly low-level investigation, done mostly with memos, a couple of phone calls, but no face-to-face visits.

Many unasked questions

An issue that Quintanilla seemed to totally overlook was the state of R.W.B.'s health. In his letter, R.W.B. wrote that following the incident, he began having "hot flashes" and felt chilled, but was also perspiring.

Did anyone even ask how the man's health had been since the incident? Could he have had radiation exposure? Did Quintanilla wonder if there was any connection to the man being in the hospital later when Hynek tried to contact him? Hynek said R.W.B. was there for a kidney stone, but did he have a history of kidney stones? Did he suffer from those before the sighting?

The witness's letter also indicated his dog didn't bark during the incident. Did he find the dog? Did the dog seem any different?

What about the herd of cattle? Were any more missing? Did R.W.B. have his cattle examined? Had there been any ill effects on them? Had they been used for meat? Could there have been a public health risk? Shouldn't Quintanilla have at least asked a veterinarian to check them out?

If any of these obvious follow-up questions were asked, there isn't any record about them in the files.

Part of scientific study

Meanwhile, the "Groveton" case file documents indicate that at least some of the paperwork from the case was also sent off to the University of Colorado for further study.

This is important to note because at the time, CU was in the middle of a two-year contract with the Air Force to do a formal study of the "unknown" sightings that had been accumulating since the late 1940s.

The final report the next year was called the *Scientific Study of Unidentified Flying Objects of the University of Colorado*. But it has come to be known as the *Condon Report*, named for the scientist who headed the scientific committee examining the *Blue Book* files.

The *Condon Report* didn't specifically mention R.W.B.'s case, despite the case being fairly new and something Condon's committee could have checked on in real time — the committee did investigate other sightings that were happening during its study. However, there's no documentation in the *Condon Report* of anyone even looking at R.W.B.'s letter to the secretary of defense.

The *Condon Report* was controversial — it claimed **Project Blue Book** wasn't providing any conclusive *scientific* evidence of UFOs.

"Our general conclusion is that nothing has come from the study of UFOs in the past 21 years that has added to scientific knowledge. Careful consideration of the record as it is available to us leads us to conclude that further extensive study of UFOs probably cannot be justified in the expectation that science will be advanced thereby."

The Condon Committee did leave the door slightly open for future study.

It said *". . . we believe that any scientist with adequate training and credentials who does come up with a clearly defined, specific proposal for study should be supported."*

The committee also said *"we think that all of the agencies of the federal government, and the private foundations as well, ought to be willing to consider UFO research proposals along with the others submitted to them on an open-minded, unprejudiced basis. While we do not think at present that anything worthwhile is likely to come of such research each individual case ought to be carefully considered on its own merits."*

The **Condon Report** provided the death knell for any follow-up government study of UFOs:

"This formulation carries with it the corollary that we do not think that at this time the federal government ought to set up a major new agency, as some have suggested, for the scientific study of UFOs. This conclusion may not be true for all time. If, by the progress of research based on new ideas in this field, it then appears worthwhile to create such an agency, the decision to do so may be taken at that time."

The **Condon Report** thus gave the Air Force top brass the prestigious scientific reason they had been seeking to be able to shut down **Project Blue Book** and get out of the public UFO business.

The last **Blue Book** cases were closed out in 1970, and the files were shipped off to Maxwell Air Force Base in Montgomery, Alabama. Over time, most of the files have been made public.

Other government documents requested by non-government UFO researchers since that time indicate that the Air Force and other agencies continued to study UFOs, although the information they collected and any reports they generated were no longer subject to public scrutiny.

One of the reasons *the* **Condon Report** was so controversial was that it apparently dismissed close encounters like the one in northwest Missouri as "unknown" and moved on.

As with the later years of **Project Blue Book**, there was a distinct bias in the *Condon Report* that extraterrestrial UFOs just couldn't be real. The committee believed that whatever it was the witness saw could have explained away, if only had been more data.

The committee's report included a strong request that teachers stop allowing their students to use books written about UFO sightings as reference material for science reports. Their goal was to strip UFO sightings of any scientific value.

That's been successful — wildly successful.

Nearly 50 years later, any book on the serious study of UFOs, including this one, won't be found in the science or military history section of any library or bookstore. Thanks to the *Condon Report*, librarians and bookstore owners now post UFO studies on the same shelves as books on the "paranormal" — alongside ghost stories, myths and legends.

You would think that those involved in the University of Colorado study would have sent out an investigator or two (they were awarded $500,000 for the study) to fly or drive a few hundred miles to northwest Missouri to get their own take on the sighting of a 100-foot diameter craft.

Indeed, after a detailed look at the Gower (Groveton) case file's documents 50 years later, an open-minded observer might wonder why the government didn't seek further evidence — and also calls into question the motives of those who wrote the *Condon Report,* who were supposed to thoroughly examine the **Blue Book** files, especially the unknowns.

It must have been very frustrating for people who reported their sightings to have had them so thoroughly dismissed.

Meanwhile, because of the response R.W.B. got the first time, its unlikely he ever contacted the Air Force again.

It would be interesting to have ask him if he ever saw the 100-foot craft again — or if any more of his cows were missing, as he said in his letter, "without a trace."

EPILOGUE

Missouri has long been known as the "Show Me" state. Many who live there are proud of that nickname. They're not gullible. They won't believe you without showing them evidence. And yet they still reported many UFO cases— including cases the Air Force wrote off as "unknown."

After 21 years and 12,618 cases — including 701 that were labeled "unidentified" or "unknown" — the Air Force shut down **Project Blue Book** in 1969. The books were finally closed in 1970. The official line was UFOs weren't a threat and didn't offer any technology that we didn't already have.

Since **Blue Book** ended, there has been no official systematic *public* U.S. government program to investigate UFOs. However, volunteer UFO researchers have long believed our government continued conducting programs to investigate UFOs — *only out of the public view.*

Facing ridicule, retired military people who said they had been sworn to secrecy began telling their stories to UFO researchers over the years. There have been numerous calls for disclosure and more congressional hearings. Over the years, none ever gained traction.

However, the lid began to open a little more in 2017.

Starting in January 2017, the CIA posted 930,000 formerly classified documents online— 12 million pages — that dated back to the 1940s when the agency was established. The documents are still being studied. Many are heavily redacted.

But in total, they reveal the truth: While telling the public to disregard UFOs, our government has been chasing after them in secret for decades. There's more.

In December 2017, the *New York Times* and *Politico* broke a story that seemed to blur the lines between science fact, science fiction, and government deep state conspiracy.

The news agencies revealed there had been at least one major UFO study after **Blue Book**. It was right out of TV's "X-files" — a black budget project called the **Advanced Aviation Threat Identification Program (AATIP).**

The story was jaw dropping. **AATIP** was secretly operated out of the Pentagon with a $22 million budget from 2007 to 2012. **AATIP (originally called Advance Aerospace Weapon System Applications Program)** was set up to study the classified military encounters with UFOs that had piled up since **Blue Book** was shut down.

They included witness accounts, Navy F/A-18 Super Hornet strike fighter gun camera footage and even strange exotic metals recovered from crash sites.

AATIP hired a private contractor, Bigelow Aerospace, to interview witnesses and scientifically research the crash debris and possibly back-engineer the technology they displayed. Bigelow set up a special warehouse or warehouses in Las Vegas to do the work and hired nearly 50 people to investigate and analyze the incidence, videos and hard evidence, according to the news accounts.

Since December 2017, there have been three military video and audio recordings of the pilots' radio communications released to the pubic. One of them is a video of a 2004 encounter with a "Tic-Tac" shaped aircraft. The three encounters show the reactions and surprise of modern-day military and civilian pilots. They can't believe what they're seeing — aircraft that defy conventional laws of physics.

The former head of **AATIP,** Luis Elizondo, has told interviewers that these unidentified craft use technology not known on Earth.

There was also a hint that more revelations from **AATIP's** now-classified material would be released. The *Washington Post* reported **AATIP** generated a 490-page volume of its findings.

With videos like those three released to the public, why was **AATIP** shut down? Elizondo said funding dried up in 2012, and he finally left the program in October 2017 out of frustration. Elizondo has since joined a for-profit company called **To The Stars Academy of Arts & Sciences**.

TTS Academy is funded by UFO enthusiast Tom DeLonge, who is the lead singer of the music group Blink-182. DeLonge hopes to continue research into unidentified aerial phenomena in hopes of tapping into their advanced technology.

A new wrinkle that could involve UFOs came out in March 2018.

Seemingly out of the blue, President Donald Trump called for adding a Space Force as a sixth branch to the U.S. military. The Pentagon has been charged with creating it.

Trump's Space Force would take on the duties of the Air Force Space Command and/or the National Reconnaissance Organization to protect the existing U.S. web of communications satellites and develop plans for "warfighting" in space.

Trump's proposal raises questions: What would a Space Force do that the Air Force can't already do with its existing technology?

Has Trump learned we already have an existing clandestine corps of pilots operating exotic spacecraft?

Will he reveal we actually have the advanced "electrogravitic" technology discussed for years in back-channel science conspiracy websites? Are these man-made UFOs what are being seen?

As of this writing in September 2018, the recent government news of UFO videos, a secret UFO study program, and a Space Force has led to growing speculation that a full disclosure of our government's activities concerning UFOs since the 1940s may be coming soon.

Meanwhile, private organizations have been continuing their own investigations for years, despite being subjected to ridicule.

Those organizations include **NICAP** (National Investigations Committee on Aerial Phenomenon, 1956-1980); **CUFOS** (J. Allen Hynek Center for UFO Studies); the **Fund for UFO Research**; and the **Mutual UFO Network** (MUFON).

MUFON tried to pick up where **Blue Book** left off. The **MUFON.com** website accepts sighting information and MUFON can send out its own trained investigators.

Most Americans don't realize the extent of information these organizations have been diligently gathering in the face of decades of ridicule after the *Condon Report* dismissed UFOs as not worthy of further study.

The reader is encouraged to examine the work of these groups, read through their books and newsletters, view their photos and videos or even attend a MUFON meeting in your area.

What should you do if you see or get a photo or video of a UFO?

You can contact police or sheriff's officers in your city, or a MUFON representative.

You can report it to the private **National UFO Reporting Center**, which operates a 24-hour hotline for sightings that happened within the last week. Both the hotline number and an online reporting form are available at the organization's website at **NUFORCE.com**.

You might also contact a local news media outlet — the old stigma of ridicule seems to be going away with all of the recent serious reports coming out of the *New York Times, the Washington Post, Politico* and major TV news networks.

What history tells us is that credible people from across the centuries all over the world have seen UFOs. And they're still seeing them on a daily basis.

MUFON reported it received 546 UFO reports in April 2018 — including 21 reports of UFOs landing, hovering, or taking off.

NUFORCE.com's recent reports includes a bright white sphere seen on June 21, 2018, in O'Fallon, Missouri:

"Driving on 64 (Highway 40) heading east to St Louis. A White (very bright Sphere approached on the south side of highway (right side of my van) at high speed, horizontal and parallel to highway. It was not coming from above, but horizontal. No contrail or light tail behind - just an extremely bright sphere. Once it passed me, it increased its speed exponentially and reduced its size and then trailed south growing smaller and extremely faster as it disappeared, it did not curve towards the earth but veered southwardly and disappeared. Increasing in speed. No sound."

Something is out there. I'm still hoping I'll get to see one myself. As the skeptics in Missouri say, show me.

About the author

Dave Toplikar is an award-winning journalist who has written tens of thousands of published stories and columns for more than three decades while based at news operations in Kansas and in Nevada. He has covered politics, government, crime, courts, fires, city hall, technology, religion, sports—and even checked into a few UFO sightings.

He was a reporter and web managing editor of the Las Vegas Sun. He was also a reporter and web managing editor at the Lawrence Journal-World.

He is now an editor at Marketing Communications, Office of Public Affairs, University of Kansas, in Lawrence, Kansas.

This is his second book on UFO sightings from **Project Blue Book.** His first, *UFO Cold Cases: Kansas, Secret USAF Files 1947-1961 Declassified*, is available on **amazon.com**. You can also see videos, his blog, and his latest Twitter posts at his website at **davetoplikarbooks.com.**

Made in the USA
Monee, IL
11 January 2025

76398822R00105